Healthy Thinking/Feeling/Doing From the Inside Out

A MIDDLE SCHOOL
CURRICULUM AND GUIDE
FOR THE PREVENTION OF VIOLENCE,
ABUSE & OTHER PROBLEM BEHAVIORS

Jack Pransky and Lori Carpenos

Healthy Thinking/Feeling/Doing
From the Inside Out

© Copyright 2000 Jack Pransky and Lori Carpenos

Developmental Editor: Euan Bear
Text Design: Sue Storey Design & Illustration
Cover Design: Sue Storey
Printing: Malloy Lithographing, Inc., Ann Arbor MI

ISBN:1-884444-60-1

Price: $28.00

Order From:

P.O. Box 340
Brandon, VT 05733
802-247-3132

Phone Orders accepted with Visa or Master Card.

CONTENTS

ABOUT THIS CURRICULUM ...

This is a curriculum for the prevention of violence, sexual abuse, substance abuse, delinquency, teenage pregnancy, teenage suicide, school disruptions, school failure and truancy and more. Yet in this curriculum, such issues are rarely tackled head-on. Instead, this curriculum attempts to intervene at the underlying, common root "cause" of all the above. In that sense it is a new and very different approach to the prevention of these problems.

The primary approach employed in this curriculum is based on a model called "Health Realization," although the curriculum itself begins with a more standard cognitive approach based on the Relapse Prevention model. Health Realization asserts that the primary, underlying cause of all the above-mentioned problems is insecurity — people acting out of insecurity — and that behind all insecurity lies insecure thinking. The problems are merely symptoms of how insecure thinking manifests itself in different people at different times.

The intent of the curriculum is to draw forth the opposite of insecurity — that is, security, which is only possible with secure, "healthy" thinking. When young people come to understand, recognize, and experience the difference between their healthy thinking and their insecure thinking and allow the infinite possibilities of healthy thinking to flow freely within them, they will be far less likely to follow their insecure thinking down problem paths into violence and other behavior problems.

The goal of this curriculum, then, is to help young people live in a state of well-being, which is the preventive antidote to all the above problems. Various names have been given to this type of generic, health-based approach, such as "internal resilience" or "prevention from the inside out."

Practitioners of Health Realization have found that people function at their healthiest when they realize the role that their thinking plays in determining their experience of life, and when they see how their thinking determines the road they travel. This curriculum is thus designed to help students have insights about the source of their health and well-being, what keeps them from experiencing it moment-to-moment, and how to get back on track. If they can gain this new perspective they will be able to monitor themselves to keep in check their insecure thinking that leads them down problem paths, until it eventually drops away as their healthy thinking intercedes and provides them with wisdom and common sense.

AUTHOR'S NOTE • PREFACE

The idea for this curriculum germinated from two relatively new ideas. A practice called Relapse Prevention (which includes elements of cognitive-behavioral treatment) has been achieving better results than usual in preventing reoffending among sexual abusers after leaving treatment, and in preventing relapse among alcohol and other drug abusers. The difference? These abusers, for the first time, learned how their own thinking created their feelings and behaviors. They learned how their distorted thinking drove them into a cycle that culminated in their abuse of others or of mood-altering substances.

Yet, people in general do not understand how their thinking is connected to their feelings and actions. Why wait to teach this understanding until after behavioral problems have already become serious? If learning about thinking and distorted thinking can affect whether abusers succumb again to problem behaviors, wouldn't it be advisable to teach this to everyone, early on, up front, as primary prevention? Wouldn't it be advisable to apply this approach to prevent violence, sexual abuse, drug dependence and other problems from occurring in the first place, or at least before the problems become serious? The entire process must be reversed, and must become proactive rather than reactive.

The second idea came through a "new" understanding about how it is possible to gain perspective on one's thinking in even more deeply influential ways than the cognitive approach guiding Relapse Prevention. Instead of trying to help people change undesirable, unhealthy or unwanted thoughts, Health Realization helps people to gain insights into how their thinking can lead them away from healthy functioning, how their own thinking gives them an experience of life out of which they then react and respond. Once people realize the power of thought in creating their lives, they see its possibilities. Their perspective shifts toward thoughts that allow them to function in healthier ways and to avoid being caught up in distorted thinking.

We believe this approach offers a breakthrough that will not only have a better chance of preventing violence, sexual abuse and substance abuse, but other behavior and learning problems. Further, it should help students function at deeper levels of well-being in all areas of their lives.

We hope you are as excited about this prospect as we are!

ACKNOWLEDGMENTS

To the following we offer the deepest thanks, for this curriculum would not have been possible without you:

To The Safer Society Foundation, Inc., of Brandon, Vermont, and to the Vermont Department of Social and Rehabilitation Services via the National Center for Child Abuse and Neglect for providing financial support for the development of this curriculum.

In memoriam to Fay Honey Knopp, for being there at the beginning with her support.

To Rob Freeman-Longo for providing material and information, and for being the general inspiration for the Relapse Prevention information in this curriculum.

To Alison Stickrod Gray for her material on "Sticky Thinking," and for her wonderful support and ideas at the beginning of this effort.

To George Pransky for his infinite wisdom and understanding of psychological functioning, and for much material gleaned for this curriculum from his masterful series of tapes on practical psychology.

To Devra Pransky for helping us to understand middle school-age student-related issues.

To the founders of Health Realization/Psychology of Mind: Dr. Roger Mills and Dr. George Pransky and their inspiration, Sydney Banks.

BEFORE YOU BEGIN:

TWO VERY IMPORTANT MESSAGES TO TEACHERS

Message 1

Using the word "curriculum" in conjunction with "Health Realization" is really a contradiction in terms. In Health Realization the only learning that counts occurs through insight — that is, whether students have their own new insights about the way they experience and respond to life. The irony is that nothing a curriculum can teach and nothing a teacher can do can *make* insights happen within another human being. No matter how clever the learning plan, no matter how brilliant the session design, no matter how exciting the learning activity, no matter how eloquent the teacher, insights can only be realized from within, and they are never guaranteed. Thus, this curriculum can only hope to point students in a direction where insights will have the best chance to occur.

What this means for teaching this Health Realization-based curriculum is that the word "curriculum" is a misnomer; it is really only a guide. The design of each session, the stories, the learning activities are only suggestions that we hope will help you, the teacher, gain your own insights about the content of each session and how it can be taught. Thus, unlike most curricula, this curriculum is not really meant to be used verbatim or taught as is — although it can be. Within the learning objectives or "the point" for each session — what we hope the students will have insights about — and based upon the suggestions offered in each session, you are encouraged to make each session your own. Each session is really meant to stimulate your own insightful ideas. More on this later.

Note: While designed for middle school, this curriculum can also be used at both the elementary and high school levels. More on this later too.

Message 2

Health Realization has found that insights have the best chance of occurring when the mind is in a calm, relaxed, clear state. The best way to ensure a calm, relaxed, clear state of mind is for students to be in a lighthearted, warm, supportive atmosphere where there is good rapport between teacher and student. This environment is most likely to occur when the teacher is in a relaxed calm, lighthearted, healthy state her or himself and when s/he sees the health in each student (more on this later too). If such a climate is not achievable or rapport is lacking, it would be inadvisable for this curriculum to be taught in that class, for it is unlikely to work under those circumstances.

THE MAIN POINTS

Ultimately, our goal is for students exposed to this curriculum to have insights about the following ideas:

- ◆ that their behaviors and feelings are connected more to their own thinking than to the circumstances or situations in which they find themselves
- ◆ that they can fall into habits of thinking that draw them into unhealthy or destructive behaviors, often without being aware of it
- ◆ that they have the ability to see and recognize this thinking in themselves and in others, thereby gaining perspective so they do not succumb as readily to it
- ◆ that they have within them natural health and intelligence, appearing in the form of insight, common sense and wisdom, and this innate health can guide them appropriately through life *if their minds are quiet enough to hear it*
- ◆ that their states of mind and feelings are their guides in helping them know whether or not they are on the right track
- ◆ that because thought is so changeable and continually creates their experience anew at every moment, they will see their lives as the continual unfolding of new hope and possibilities.

HOW TO USE THIS CURRICULUM

The intent of this curriculum is for students to have insights about the "Key Points" listed in each session, so that these understandings will constructively affect their lives. To achieve greatest impact, the students must see how these understandings play out in their own lives.

Although this entire curriculum was designed to bring about insight, understanding and changes in thoughts, feelings and behaviors, we recognize that the activities or stories we've chosen within each session may or may not be the best way for you, the teacher, to help students gain these understandings. The activities and stories depicted here represent the authors' best thinking (at the time of writing this curriculum) about how to help students learn and incorporate these ideas. As suggested earlier, once you as teacher begin to gain these understandings for yourself, you will likely create new and better ways to teach these. In fact, this is advisable because they will be your own creations; therefore, you will likely teach them with more heart.

Thus, the best way to use his curriculum is as a guide that provides the foundation from which to create your own activities to best convey the Key Points to your students.

Alternatively, this curriculum offers straight "lesson plans" for each session, complete with activities and stories. The first time around, you as a teacher may feel more comfortable adhering closely to the sessions as written, and in subsequent sessions when your comfort level has risen you may then want to create your own activities or stories, as your own level of understanding deepens and new ideas naturally appear for you.

If for any session you feel that you have not gained as deep an understanding of any lesson as you would like before having to teach it, that is okay. In that case you are encouraged to say to the students that you will both be learning this together as a partnership. In fact, that could be the case for the entire curriculum.

However creatively you teach the lessons, it is probably best to stay close to the Key Points to be learned for each session, since having insights about these is the intent of the curriculum. However, as your level of understanding deepens you may find even new and better ways to express these points, and you may find better ways to help the points "hit home" or become real to the students.

An Alternative:
Using Open-ended Discussion Questions
to Draw Out Student Insights

Rather than proceed through each of these lesson plans as written or using these lessons to inspire their own lesson plans, some teachers may find it more advisable to simply engage students in open-ended discussions to help draw out their own insights about each of these issues.

For teachers who choose to teach the curriculum in this way, each session contains a box with one or more open-ended questions. Here, the teacher may want to simply get the students in a reflective frame of mind, ask them one of these questions, and engage students in an open-ended discussion where, through their reflections, they come up with their own answers about the issue at hand. The questions listed are by no means the only questions that may be asked; they merely serve as examples of the types of questions that may stimulate reflective discussion. It is hoped that through the act of reflection, students will come to their own insights.

We believe that having students go into reflection and engage in reflective discussion may be one of the best ways to help students have personal insights concerning the topic's relevance to their own lives. Certainly it is better than having someone "tell them" about the issue, and it may even be better or at least as good as hoping they will gain insights through a story or exercise. Remember, this curriculum is based on insight learning. Rather than try to change thoughts or behaviors after they've already been formed, this curriculum seeks to point people to new understandings or new ways of using their thinking so they can create new thoughts and new, healthier behaviors. This perspective sets it apart from most other prevention curricula; it is the reason this curriculum is relevant for *all* problem behaviors instead of tackling them one at a time. When an insight occurs at a deep level pertaining to basic principles of mental health and well-being, such learning is naturally and automatically generalized to other areas of life.

The questions we have offered are intended to help the student focus on what to look for, giving them practice in a learning method that can be applied to all topic areas. If students begin any session by asking themselves a question and going into reflection about it, they will find that their focus and concentration will increase. Furthermore, this method of learning gives students practice in critical thinking. The sooner students develop this skill, the better off they will be. Young people who know they can rely on their own capacity for common sense, wisdom, and good judgment are less likely to succumb to peer pressure as readily as their less secure peers.

A caution is in order in applying the curriculum in this way, however. If students do not feel a high enough trust level with the teacher, they may not be in the frame of mind needed to open themselves to this kind of reflective learning. If the students are acting too immature in the moment, they may not be in the frame of mind necessary for this kind of learning. The wisdom of the teacher, which arises from the teacher's own reflective frame of mind, should be the determining factor in how to apply this curriculum.

Finally, for teachers who decide to try this reflective discussion approach as the means for teaching any of these lessons, it would be very wise to first read through the lesson plan a few times to see what its intended learnings are before attempting to engage students in this kind of discussion. The teacher should then reflect on the questions. By doing so, the teacher will know better what to say in response to students when needed. The pre-presentation review and personal reflection time may help the teacher to come up with other questions that may be even better than those offered here. Also, it may be advisable, where possible, to seat students in a circle for this kind of discussion, provided there are not too many students.

A suggested process to use is as follows: 1) the teacher asks the students to quiet their minds; 2) the teacher then asks the class a reflective question; 3) the students are asked to quietly reflect on the answer for themselves; 4) any student who is ready may offer her or his answer to the group, speaking only about what it looks like or feels like to himself or herself; 5) the other students are asked to listen deeply to what each student says, without judging what anyone has to say, so that the speaker's answer may trigger reflective responses from other students. The intention is for the discussion to keep going deeper, as more students gain insights. The teacher simply keeps the discussion on track and offers any personal insights when it seems right in the discussion.

To set up this kind of discussion initially, the teacher may want to say something like this before starting: "The purpose of a discussion like this is for you to find your own answers to questions you are about to hear. There are no right or wrong answers, only what you find to be true for you. At times I may tell you what I have found to be true for myself, but that may not be helpful to you. What each person has discovered or learned for himself or herself is only really useful to that person. The path to this discovery is called reflection. Reflection means to quietly consider or have a look at things within the context of your own life. Through reflection, people are able to draw upon their own common sense and wisdom, which is always available to you if you know where to find it. Sometimes people have wonderful insights through reflection. Having insights means seeing something that is very helpful to you from somewhere deep inside of you. It doesn't come from what someone else thinks, or even from what you have thought in the past. An insight is like realizing something new and fresh, something you may not have considered before, but once you see it, it will look so obvious to you that you'll wonder why you hadn't realized it before. Then, once you have these insights, if you share them with others, it might help to trigger something in them that may help lead them to their own insights.

"Here is how you can prepare yourself to have insights and to bring out your common sense: it simply takes quieting down your mind. If you're going too fast with a bunch of old, familiar thoughts, you're not likely to have new insights. So we're talking about resting your mind and being curious about what might pop into your mind at any moment. It is also a good idea to get into a place of 'not knowing.' What this means is to resist thinking you know the answer before you've really reflected on it. It's too easy and too tempting to jump to conclusions or rely on something that was a good idea in the past but really doesn't apply now. So, slowing down, quieting your mind, and being willing to not know the answer until it occurs to you out of the blue is a good way to approach each of these sessions. This doesn't mean that you will always get an insight, so never expect one. Never be disappointed if you don't. Then you'll be in a good frame of mind to reflect on the questions posed at the beginning of each session. In fact, we've found that getting into this reflective mode of thinking is helpful whenever we want to settle down, take in new information, and increase our ability to be present and attentive. It certainly can't hurt!"

THE FOUNDATION FOR TEACHING THIS CURRICULUM

We begin with some assumptions:

1. Ultimately, we are striving for students to think in healthier, more productive ways, and for that thinking to affect their behavior in healthier, more productive ways.

2. For this new thinking to be realized, the learning that occurs through this curriculum must truly take hold; in other words, the learning must become part of them, or it will not make much difference. This curriculum is thus designed in accordance with what research says best aids learning[1], as follows:

   ◆ to have learning occur in an environment of utmost respect for the learner — in a warm, caring, lighthearted, supportive, compassionate atmosphere, with good rapport between teacher and students;

   ◆ to have leaning related to the student's own experience and relevant to their lives — to have it touch people's own lives;

   ◆ to have learning be immediately applied;

   ◆ to have learning occur through direct experience (that people retain 20% of what they hear; 40% of what they hear and see; and 80% of what they experience)

The first step, then, is to create an environment of utmost respect that draws out the students' natural health and wisdom. In other words, when students are treated as the teacher would like to be treated — with utmost respect — students will have a greater tendency to respond in kind.

---

[1]Adapted from Knowles, M., 1989.

CURRICULUM STRUCTURE AND FORMAT

This curriculum includes 26 sessions that can be conducted either once a week for 26 consecutive weeks, or two sessions per week over 14 weeks, or over 26 consecutive days, or within one full, continuous week. In other words, we have tried to create a curriculum with the maximum flexibility that can best fit into the structure of each different school and classroom. Whatever structure will best fit best into the teacher's schedule is fine.

Each session has been designed to fit into a 30- to 50-minute time period. However, some sessions may run overtime because there is no way to predict the extent of involvement in student discussions for each session. Where student participation is high, the teacher may continue the session into the time period of the following session.

Each session is presented in the following format:

A. To teachers

an opening statement to teachers describing what the session is attempting to get across

B. Key Points

the crux of the issue that it is hoped students will walk away understanding

C. Needed Materials

for the particular session

D. Opening Statement

for students

E. Activity

each session's main activity or story line

F. Home Practice

assignment

G. Summary

summary or conclusion statement to help drive the point home

In addition, prototypes for overheads or drawings and any handouts for that session are provided at the end of that session.

Before teaching each session, it is advisable for you to read the entire session over two or three times, then sit with it and see if any insights arise from your own life. You can then use some of these insights to help illustrate your points. Insights may arise about better ways to teach it. Then you can fit it all together and go to it! Or you can teach it as is.

This curriculum has been designed so that each session builds upon the ones before it. Purposeful repetition is built in to ensure that the understanding takes hold. Wherever repetition does occur the session is designed to take that point one step further or deeper. To jump into the middle of the curriculum to teach a session may do a disservice because the students will not have the foundation that grounds it. Yet, since the only learning that counts here comes through individual insight, even this logic is up for grabs. However, we are not recommending that people simply pluck out random sessions to teach.

In addition, although this curriculum was designed for the middle school, it can be also used as a guide to teach this material in either high school or elementary school. It has relevance in both directions. The points to be learned are the same, though for elementary school they may need to be stated in a simpler way. Some of the activities and stories can be used for younger or older students as is, but others will have to be adjusted. As an example, an elementary school guidance counselor named Katie Kelley has demonstrated the difference between conditioned thinking and clear thinking by filling a glass with water and mud, and shaking it up (our "mud mind"), then letting it settle (our "clear mind"). Tiny little kids can understand the difference. There is no limit to the ingenuity of a teacher with a clear mind.

THE BASIC PHILOSOPHY BEHIND THIS APPROACH

If students were to behave from a state of well-being they would not behave in troublesome or troubled ways. They would be wholly attentive to learning, and their learning capacity would be at its peak. This is the state we are striving for.

This curriculum begins with the premise that this state of health or well-being, or at least the capacity to achieve it, exists naturally within all students. It can never be destroyed. The only reason that students do not act as if they have this innate health and common sense is because of the way they have come to think. Certain ways of thinking, which children inadvertently pick up as they grow, obscure this natural state of health — sometimes so powerfully that people can lose sight of it altogether. But it is never really gone, and it can be tapped or drawn out in anyone, even in the most troubled or troubling students.

Students (and teachers) behave according to how they think. If their thinking arises from their health, they will naturally behave in healthy ways. If their thinking arises from some unhealthy conditioning that they picked up, they will behave according to whatever "distortions" are part of this thinking. We don't often see how our thinking affects us. We simply follow it as if it is "real," because it is all we can see at the time. Students' behaviors follow their thinking.

The question becomes, "How can we help students to behave and learn out of their wise, healthy thinking state instead of out of their unwise, unproductive thinking state?" Practitioners of Health Realization found that if it weren't for the distorted, problematic, habitual thinking that young people (and all of us) get caught up in, they would naturally act out of their healthy, wise, responsive thinking — for this health is their natural state. Students (and teachers) can regain this natural state of health by slowing down or clearing away their unnatural, unhealthy thinking. In the absence of such thinking, healthy thinking naturally emerges. It pops up when our minds are relaxed.

The basis for this model can be found in the discovery of three principles whose interplay determines how we experience life. In other words, what we see as "life" can be boiled down to three principles we call "Mind," "Consciousness," and "Thought."

In this context "Mind" refers to the intelligence behind life — the "life force" that gives us the energy to exist and to function in life. Mind is the source of two gifts, two awesome powers that we have been given to create our lives with.

One such gift is the power of Thought. Thought is, essentially, the power to create. No creation in history did not begin with Thought. With this faculty of Thought we have an unlimited capacity to create thoughts in the form of images and ideas. With this power of Thought we have the continual capacity to create anew at every moment. If we look closely we can see that most of our thoughts just come to us; we don't try to think them. They just seem to appear in our consciousness.

Our other gift is the power of Consciousness. Consciousness is, essentially, the power to experience. The startling discovery embodied in Health Realization is that our consciousness is capable of experiencing only one thing: what we create through our thinking.

This means that the only experiences in life that we can have are what our consciousness picks up from our thinking. What looks to us as if it is being directly perceived by our senses is really being instantly altered by our thinking before it even registers in our brain. In other words, we cannot have any experience of the outside world, except as it appears to us through our thinking. This is why people in the same room looking in the same direction will notice different things, why some people like certain smells and others don't, why we might not feel the pain of a cut at one moment and do at other moments, why we might not hear a clock ticking until someone calls it to our attention, why people's tastes differ. Thus, we cannot be directly conscious of "the real world"; we can only experience our own reality as filtered or interpreted already through our own thinking. Another way of saying it is that our experience of life is really an inside-out affair, even though it looks as if our experience is coming to us from outside of ourselves, from our circumstances, from the situations we find ourselves in, or from what other people do to us.

Because of the ever-present flow of Thought within us, and the fact that the thoughts that flow through are so fluid and changeable, we find that our perceived reality is also far more fluid and changeable than most of us have come to believe. And therein lies the power and the hope to create change in our lives — if we can truly realize what is really going on and how it all works.

For example, when we have a problem most of us tend to blame something in the outside world, or we tend to look to change something in the outside world in order to fix it. Yet, we find that by looking inside to the true source of our experience, to our own thinking and to the realization that this thinking changes and can change again, we gain a truly awesome power to change our experience, in fact our very lives, toward health, for this health, this wisdom and intelligence, is naturally and continually flowing within us. Thus, we don't need to do anything to find this health and wisdom. All we need to do is not allow the thoughts that keep us from experiencing this healthy part of ourselves to get in its way.

We have the power to rise above what we think we know, and there is no limit to this understanding. To truly understand that what we see as "real" is only thought, and it is different for everyone, and thought can change, seems to be enough to give hopeless people hope and turn around lives of despair — if it is realized through one's own insight.

Every person has the capacity to realize this healthy flow of thinking within us, and to realize the kind of thinking that keeps us from experiencing it. We even have a built-in mechanism that tells us whether we are on or off track (of our health), called our feelings and emotions. These are signals that tell us how far away from our health we are at any moment. We only have to listen to them and make adjustments.

This approach does not negate the fact that things happen to us in the outside world over which we have little or no control. Some things that happen most people would call terrible and harmful. Yet, when we realize that some people even take in those experiences differently through their own thinking, and that we even think about those occurrences and events differently at different times, a new world of possibilities opens before us. Our thoughts allow us to either stay in a negative experience or to overcome it in ways we haven't yet been able to imagine. Such is the power of thought. It can turn around lives — if its power is truly realized.

Obviously, it is not enough to just say these words and expect them to have any real meaning for people — unless it is personally experienced. This is what this curriculum hopes to achieve with students.

In summary, through this curriculum we hope that students will have insights where they come to realize that they have health in them that they can rely on to guide them, how their own thinking often inadvertently gets in the way of this health, how they can find the healthy flow of thinking within them whenever their busy thinking calms down, how they are capable at any moment of having new thoughts and therefore new experiences, and how this new perspective can be used to guide them well and productively in school and for the rest of their lives. As a result, students who gain this understanding function at higher levels of well-being.

A note to the teacher: don't worry if this explanation made little sense to you or if it had no meaning for you. The purpose of the entire curriculum is to help it make sense, to help its meaning come alive. If it is new to you, you can join the students in the process of discovery. And training is available if you want to understand it more before you begin (see end of Bibliography in the Appendix).

Session One

Why We Behave As We Do

A. To Teachers

Remember, before you start, set the stage! Be sure the atmosphere in the room is calm, comfortable, lighthearted, warm, supportive, and that you have established good rapport with your students. Remind yourself of this process before each session.

The purpose of this session is to help students look at their behavior, not as something that just seems to happen, but as something that emerges from their thinking. Most students tend to see their behaviors in reaction to certain events or situations or issues. The idea is for students to recognize their thinking as the starting point and, therefore, as the point of departure.

Before tackling this, the session attempts to help the students prepare themselves mentally to listen to this entire series. The more that they can open themselves to new ideas the more effective the curriculum will be. Students need to be prepared for a different kind of listening than they are used to — listening from the heart instead of through their intellect; listening for the heart of the message rather than for content. Young people often find this easier to do than adults.

Sample Questions for Reflective Discussion

What do you think magical listening would be like?

What do you think your listening would be like if it were magical?

Where do you think our behavior comes from? Trace it to the source. (Note: if they say, "our brain," ask, "What do you think would make a behavior come into our brain?")

Why do you think people behave badly sometimes?

When we behave in ways that cause problems for ourselves or others, what do you think is the source of that behavior? Where does it come from?

B. Key Points

◆ To best gain the jewels of understanding from this course, it is best to listen with a quiet mind and a clear head, so the ideas can gently sift in and perhaps strike a chord inside, to listen not to the content of the words but for the feeling behind the words, to listen not by judging but by stepping back and observing. (In fact, this is a helpful way to listen to everyone.)

◆ Though we are not often aware of it, a thought always lies behind every behavior.

◆ When we behave in ways that cause problems for ourselves or others, the real culprit is our thoughts.

C. Needed Materials

An open mind.

D. Opening Statement for Students

Have you ever wondered what it would be like to be able to do magical listening?[1]

ASK: What do you think magical listening would be like? What do you think it would be like if you were able to listen to something with magical ears? What do you think you would hear?

[discussion]

It transports us like magic right into what another person is saying so that we can see it or feel it like they see it or feel it. But to do it, we can't have anything else on our minds. When other thoughts come into our minds that are getting in the way of our magical listening, we just want to let them go. This is the kind of listening we hope that you will be able to use to listen to the jewels of understanding that lie within this curriculum.

Everyone please close your eyes and relax. Get comfortable in your chairs. Take a deep breath, and let it out slowly.

Take another, fill your lungs way up slowly, and let your breath out slowly.

One more time. Deep breath. Fill lungs. Slowly let the air out. Now, just let a peaceful, quiet feeling rest over you. If any thoughts come into your mind, just let them peacefully pass. Let them go. (Let the students stay in that peace for about 30 seconds).

(Then, very softly, say something like this:) Now please keep your eyes closed while I'm talking for a moment. Enjoy the peacefulness.

[Note: If a student makes a wisecrack or tries to do something to get attention, the teacher could say something like: "Oh, I hear someone trying to break our peace. That is understandable. We are so used to having our minds racing at 90 miles an hour that it can sometimes feel uncomfortable at first to do this. But when our minds slow down enough we find that everyone has this peaceful place inside them, and the people who slow their thinking down enough to listen for it will find treasures that they never thought of before. It's there for everyone who wants it." And if the students still do not stop, the teacher could continue with something like: "But even if someone isn't ready yet to find this peace, it would not really be fair of him (or her) to try to interfere with everyone else's peace,

---

[1]The term magical listening was coined by Debra Crosby of Lynn, Massachussetts.

would it? All we're asking is for everyone to give it an equal try. There are no right or wrong answers in this curriculum. Everyone is on an equal footing. The wise people will want to find out what they can discover for themselves."]

For a moment we're going to talk about how to listen during these sessions. It's not the kind of listening that we usually ask you to do in school. Usually we try to fill our heads with all the information we're getting, and we learn how to analyze that information. That's not how you want to listen to these sessions.

Here, in these sessions, instead of filling your mind with the information and facts that you hear, you want to do the opposite. Empty your mind. You want to have nothing on your mind. Listen out of the peacefulness of a quiet mind. You want to listen to this like you listen to music. Just get a feel for it. There is no need to take notes. With an open mind what is being talked about here will probably start to make sense to you. If it does you might naturally begin to think about things in a way you've never quite thought of before. Just let it happen. There are no right or wrong answers here. Whatever makes sense to you is the only learning that counts here — whatever feels right to you in your heart; whatever rings true for you. But the path to this type of learning is an open mind, having nothing on your mind. That's all you have to bring to these sessions. If you do, it may even be fun!

Okay, slowly, you can open your eyes now.

Are you ready? Try to stay in that quiet, peaceful place as much as possible while you're listening and responding to this session.

This course is all about knowing that every one of us has a power within us that gives us what we experience in life, and how knowing what that power is and how to access it, can guide our lives in healthy ways, and can give us the experience we want in life.

Right now those are just words. They don't mean anything. The whole purpose of this curriculum is to help us see the meaning behind those words so our lives can be the way we want.

So here goes …

If you really take a look at it, behavior is a funny thing. It looks like people just act.

For example, if someone knocks your books off the desk, it looks as if he or she has just done it out of nowhere. But if you look at this action closely, you will see that something is always behind the behavior. Something makes that behavior happen. Today, we're going to see what that something is.

E. Activity/Story Line

ASK: Have you ever wondered what makes your friends act the way they do? Think about your friends or the other students you see around the school. Give me some words that describe how each one usually acts — no names, just words about how they act.

[Write these down on the board as a brainstormed list.]

[Use what the students said (what is written on the board) to summarize. So it may come out something like this:] So you're saying that—

> one of your friends might act tough.
>
> one of your friends might act like a pussycat.
>
> one of your friends might act smart.
>
> one of your friends might act stupid.
>
> one of your friends might act like a crybaby.
>
> one of your friends might act cool.

Have you ever wondered why?

Have you ever wondered why you act differently than they do?

Well — ta da dah!

There is an answer!

The answer is, they act differently because — THEY THINK DIFFERENTLY!!!

Actions and behaviors come from the way we think.

To put it another way, behind every action lies a thought, or set of thoughts.

Sometimes those thoughts go by so fast we can't even tell they're there.

**Faster than a
speeding bullet!**

Let's look at a couple of examples:

If your action is playing basketball, somewhere before that happened, you had a thought:

"I think I'll shoot some hoops." or —

"Sounds good, shoot some hoops."

or something like that.

ASK: Do you think it's possible to play basketball without having some kind of thought like that?

[If they say no]: Interesting, isn't it? Without that thought, you wouldn't be playing basketball because you wouldn't have the thought to do it.

[If they say yes], ask: Well, tell me how would you get to the basketball court? How would your legs take you there? Those are thoughts!

Suppose a teacher asks a question in class, and you raise your hand. Sometimes this happens so fast you don't even notice it, but before that hand goes up you might think:

"Hey! I know the answer. Call on me!" or —

"Maybe I know this." or —

"Maybe I can fool the teacher into thinking I know this."

Or something like that.

ASK: Okay, name some actions or behaviors — any behaviors.

[List 10 or so on the board. You may hear things like eating, drinking, dressing, fighting, studying. Smart-alecks may say, "having sex." Then ask the following question for each answer on the list:]

ASK: What might be some possible thoughts behind each of these?

[If their answers make sense to you, they will make sense to them. If the answers don't make sense to you, ask what they mean.]

ASK: Try to think of a behavior that doesn't have a thought behind it.

[In response, here are a couple of possibilities that you might hear: "Punching somebody." Ask something like: "How would you make your arm move if you didn't have a thought?" In response the student may say, "I just felt it" or "I felt like it." Ask: "Where did the feeling come from? What made you have the feeling?" In response the student may say that someone did something to them. Ask: "Well, would everyone react exactly the same way?" "What makes the difference?" "The difference is that people have different thoughts about it that cause different reactions."]

No action (except for a physical reflex like a knee-jerk or breathing, heart pumping), no behavior, can exist without a thought coming first.

ASK: Have you ever wondered what makes your friends feel the way they do? For example:

> At different times your friend might feel happy.

> At different times your friend might feel sad.

> At different times your friend might feel mad.

> At different times your friend might feel afraid.

ASK: What other ways might your friends feel at different times?

[Continue the list.]

ASK: Do you think that thoughts might come before feelings too, just like thoughts come before actions?

Wouldn't that be something!

What if you feel like having an ice cream cone? If you say to yourself: "Yeah, ice cream! Cool." that's a thought. So at least some feelings have thoughts behind them.

What if someone feels angry? Suppose your friend's computer just ate her homework, and she feels like throwing it across the room. Does that feeling have a thought behind it?

What if you wanted to be with a certain boy or girl and he or she didn't want to be with you. You might feel pain, but the thought behind it might be: "Ohhhh, that hurts." Or "Maybe I'm not attractive enough," Or, "What am I going to do now?" Or, "So what, I deserve better than that stuck up so-and-so."

What if your friend feels really bad about problems at home? The thought behind it might be: "My dad doesn't care about me" or "I wish I could be adopted" or "I can't wait 'til I can be on my own."

All these are thoughts that are behind the feelings. But they go by so fast that we don't see them. All we are left with are the feelings. We think we feel the way we do because of situations or circumstances that happen to us, but really it's our own thinking that causes our reactions.

What if someone feels sad but they don't know why? That person may not know what she's thinking, but maybe she's thinking something deep inside that she doesn't know about or that she doesn't realize she's thinking about.

It's the same with being happy or any of those feelings.

So at the very least we could say, maybe feelings have a thought behind them too.

Wow! All actions, all behaviors, and all feelings have thoughts behind them.

ASK: Why do you think this discussion might be important in your lives?

[discussion]

[Note to teacher: If the students don't have a clue, say something like:"All we have to know at this point is that no matter what we are feeling or how we are acting we are always thinking something that's behind it." And the significance of that is what the concluding statement says below.

F. Home Practice

Over the next day (or week or whatever) watch your thoughts. When you *act* a certain way, see if you can see the thought behind it. When you *feel* a certain way see if you can see what the thought is behind it. Write down 5 things that you did over the week or 5 times you felt some feelings or emotions and the thoughts that were behind them.

G. Summary/Conclusion

If thinking lies behind behaviors and feelings, we can't really do anything about behaviors and feelings unless we do something about the thinking. That is our starting point!

Session Two
The Thought-Feeling-Behavior Chain

A. To Teachers

In the last session we introduced the concept of "thought." The purpose of this session is to help the students understand the importance of thought in their own lives.

Ironically, thought is something we usually do not think about. It just happens. But short of breathing (which we usually don't think about either), thought is probably the most important thing we do in life. Why? Our thinking often controls us without our knowing it. In other words, thought makes us do things. It makes us behave in certain ways. It makes us feel certain things.

Let us examine more closely how our feelings and behaviors flow from our thinking. For example, let's say our behavior is walking to the kitchen to get some chocolate cake. What lies behind this behavior? Perhaps we had a craving for chocolate. What might lie behind this feeling? Somewhere along the line we must have had a thought such as: "I really want something sweet. Not just sweet, oooh, yeah, chocolate." Then we feel it! Thought makes us feel it, and thought makes us do it — only most of the time we don't realize it. It starts out with an innocent thought. We just do it, and then we notice the results of what we've done. The same is true for all our behaviors. The same is true for others' behaviors.

To recognize the power that thought has in our lives and how it helps create our experience of life is one of the most empowering things we can know.

Given that thoughts are behind all our behavior, the more we understand the nature of "thought" the better able we will be to influence the effect thought has on us. The answers to why we behave as we do are within us. We only have to realize it.

B. Key Points

◆ We behave and act in certain ways because of what we feel; behind the feelings are thoughts.

◆ Thoughts, feelings and behaviors form a cycle; just as a bicycle chain is made up of links, our feelings and our behaviors are linked to our thoughts.

C. Needed Materials

A picture of a chain with links.

A picture of a bicycle chain (or a clean actual bicycle chain).

A diagram of the thought-feeling-behavior cycle.

A diagram of an example of the thought-feeling-behavior cycle at work.

  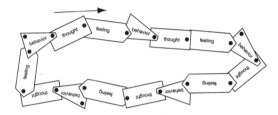

Sample Questions for Reflective Discussion

What happens inside you when you get nervous about taking a test?

Where do those feelings come from?

What do you think could be so powerful that it can either give us wonderful feelings or terrible feelings?

How do you think a person would feel if they wanted to beat somebody up?

D. Opening Statement

Today we're going to dig a little deeper into the nature of thought and how it affects feelings and behaviors.

ASK: In your practice at home, since the last session, what did you notice about thinking in your lives?

[brief discussion]

Thoughts sometimes set off a chain reaction that makes us feel things and do things. That's how powerful thoughts are. In this session we're going to see how this works.

E. Activity/Story Line

Let's say that all of a sudden we have a craving for a pizza — a nice, luscious, steamy, mouth-watering, scrumptious, the best crust, our favorite topping PIZZA.

Does it make you want one?

How many of you can feel your mouth watering right now?

Isn't that interesting? There is no real pizza in sight. It is only a thought. Yet it has this power to make our senses feel it. When we have a thought of pizza, that thought sometimes makes us want one.

It may be making you want one right now.

Or maybe your thoughts are making you not want to be here, in this class, right now. Either experience is only a thought.

No matter what we are feeling right now, no matter what we want to do, our thoughts are making us feel it.

This is the power of thought in our lives. In fact, nothing is more powerful. Thought is the most awesome power we have — and we usually don't realize it.

A thought is so powerful it can make us taste it — like the pizza. It can make us salivate.

Or if you're not salivating, that means you're having different thoughts, or you don't like pizza!

Let's consider the people who do not want to be here right now. That too is a thought. Some people want to be here; others do not. The only difference in what each of us is experiencing is the thought.

Or let's say we're about to take a test. We might feel it in the stomach.

Or we don't and are just relaxed about the test.

The only difference is our thoughts about it.

If the test was actually causing the bad-feeling stomach, everybody would feel the same way.

But some don't.

That's because they have different thoughts — about the test.

Those thoughts make them feel differently about it.

If a test is gnawing at our stomachs, what we're really feeling is our own thoughts about the test gnawing at our stomach.

What about something really serious that makes you upset? What are some of those things?

[Brainstorm a list. If abuse is not on the board, add it]

Let's take abuse. If we've been abused in the past, the thought of it may make our stomach tighten or make us feel sick.

But if it is not happening right at this moment, that too is only our own thoughts making us feel that way right now.

That's how powerful thoughts are.

They can get us to feel anything.

ASK: Think about a time when you felt physical pain. How did you get the pain? [brainstorm another, short list: broken bones, bicycle accident, fell out of a tree, sports injury] Can you almost feel the pain right now?

How many of you can imagine what the pain felt like?

What you're feeling right now is the thought — only the thought.

More accurately, the thought is making you feel the feeling.

But it's still only a thought.

Amazing, isn't it? Powerful little critters, aren't they?

ASK: Think of the time when you felt the most wonderful. Can you almost feel it now?

That's just the thought too.

Here's how it all works:

ASK: Picture a bicycle. What makes the bicycle go?

[entertain ideas and display picture of the bicycle and chain]

We could pedal it, but if no chain were attached to the pedals and wheels, it would not move — you know what happens when you're truckin' along up a steep hill and the chain falls off. So without the chain, the bike would not move.

Let's look closely at the chain. A chain is make up of a series of links, all connected together, in a (sort of) circle. It's not really a circle but it goes around and around and it has no openings. It's like a cycle that repeats itself over and over.

Any time we act or behave in any way, something is happening inside of us like the bicycle chain.

Let's go back to the pizza example. Suppose we find ourselves eating that pizza. How did that behavior happen?

Let's look at the links of the chain that got us there.

1. First, something may have triggered a thought. In this case it may have been because we were just talking about pizza. It comes in through at least one of our senses. In this case, our ears heard talk about pizza or our eyes saw the word "pizza."

2. But before that outside trigger even registers in our brains (because we might not even be aware of it in the first place), instantly we get a thought, something like: "Pizza! I'm really hungry!"

3. Next we might get a feeling of hunger in our stomach.

4. Next we might have another thought: "I think I'll stop and get a slice on the way home."

5. Before we know it we have the behavior of eating pizza.

6. Then we experience the results of it: a full stomach.

That's how it happens.

That's kind of how all our behaviors happen.

Here is a diagram of how it happens.

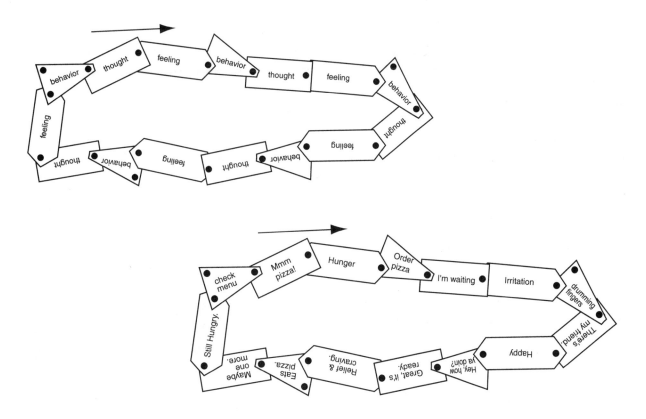

If any one link breaks, the chain breaks, the cycle breaks, and the behavior doesn't happen.

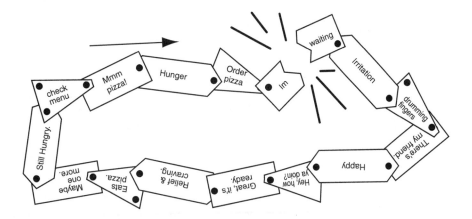

Or a different behavior happens.

ASK: What links do you think could break the pizza chain?

[Refer to diagram during this brief discussion. Note to teachers: Students may say that they can break the chain at the behavior link by having the willpower not to eat the pizza. But if they look closer they will see that willpower is really nothing more than a set of thoughts. It always comes back to thought.]

We have the power within us to break the chain at any of the thought links, and then the whole cycle stops. We won't be able to change how we act or change how we feel unless our thinking changes.

Alternate or Additional Activity

Remember in the last session we went into peaceful silence for a while? Let's do that again, but this time I want you to pay attention to the thoughts. In other words I want you to observe your thoughts.

Our thoughts come into our heads even though we don't want them to.

ASK: So here is what I want you to do. Close your eyes. Like before, take three deep breaths — slowly — holding in the air, and letting it out real slowly. The idea is to keep your mind as free and clear as possible so you can experience that peacefulness. But just in case any thoughts creep into your head, just notice what they are, and then let them go. Okay? Begin.

[After about 45 seconds of silence, bring them gently out of it.]

ASK: Did anyone not have any thoughts at all?

[It is virtually impossible for people to have no thoughts, so if a student says he didn't, he is either pulling your leg or is completely unaware of his thinking or maybe what even constitutes thinking.]

We all have thoughts pop in — even when we don't want them to.

ASK: Where do thoughts come from that we don't try to think?

[entertain ideas]

We don't really know. Obviously, they come from inside us. But are they manufactured in our brain? How would our brains come up with a new thought that it never had before? It's a mystery. It almost seems as if there is a flow of thinking that runs through us like a stream that we're not really aware of, and it is so powerful that we can't stop it even if we wanted it to.

That's how powerful our thinking is.

ASK: What did you notice about your own thinking? What did your thinking look like to you? I don't mean what were your specific thoughts, but what were the kinds of things that your thinking did? What was your thinking like? Where did it go? Where did it take you?

[From the students' responses, list the qualities or characteristics of thinking on the board. You may hear responses such as, "they just kept coming and I couldn't stop them," or, "I heard a noise," or "I thought about something I had to do," or "I thought about my dog," or "I just kept hearing this commercial running through my head" or "I started thinking about trying to stop my thinking," etc.]

These are some of the kinds of thoughts we have that distract us without our usually being aware of them. It's so much a part of us and so close to us that most of the time we don't even realize we're thinking at all. But it still gives us an experience — in other words, a lot of those thoughts take us away from the peacefulness we were trying to feel — whether we're aware of them or not.

ASK: Do you think a fish is aware of the water it swims in?

[brief discussion]

It's hard to think like a fish, but a fish is so close to the water that he probably doesn't even see it — unless he jumps out. That's just like our thinking. We're so close to it that we don't see most of it. Only we can never jump out of our thinking.

ASK: How many of you were able to let go of the thoughts that came into your head? Raise your hands.

[Maybe no one was able to let go of them. But even if one student was able to, ask—]

ASK: How did you let go of them? Can you tell us?

[entertain ideas]

Maybe we can even practice letting go of thoughts we don't want, even when we're not trying to be peaceful — just anytime our thoughts interfere with us. Wow, wouldn't that be something!

F. Home Practice

[If they did the first activity:] Think about one behavior that you do in school or at home. Think about what the thought-feeling-behavior links are. Write down 5 things you did, the feelings behind them, and the thoughts you had either when you did them or just before you did them.

[Or/and, if they did the alternate activity:] When you're at home, any time you think about it, notice your thinking, and see if you can let go of the thoughts you don't want.

G. Summary/Conclusion

Our behaviors do not just happen. Feelings and behaviors are the result of thoughts. It sometimes looks as if the chain is set in motion by something in the environment, but the real mover is our own thoughts, because the same event will not cause the same response in different people. Most of our thinking is not intentional. Only a little of it do we go out of our way to think. The trick is to know what to do with it, which we will discuss in later sessions.

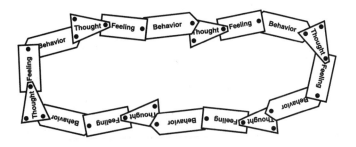

Session Three

Perceptions And Thoughts

A. To Teachers

In the last session we introduced the concept of the thought-feeling-behavior chain and how it creates a cycle. In this session we're going to look a little more closely at some of the components of the chain, and how they interrelate.

The idea in this session is to help the student relate to thought in its most simple form — as a baby might think when s/he enters the world — to help the student understand how thought begins to come out differently in people and affect his or her world. Our "world" comes out differently depending on how we come to think.

This may be a complex point, so an important distinction must be made here. Of course the "real world" exists. It hits our five senses. Yet, in truth, we can know nothing of what our senses are picking up except through our own thinking. In other words, our thinking intercedes at the very instant of sensory impact. We can only sense and experience the outside world through our own thinking.

As an example of how this works, some intensity of light may impact our eyeballs, but the moment we experience it as "light," or the moment we sense a particular brightness or color, our thoughts have already taken over. In other words, what we have picked up through our eyeballs is really our own thinking, and not the "real thing." If something hits our sense of touch, the moment we feel it and it feels soft or hard or sharp, our thoughts have already interceded. The same is true for all our senses. Thus, all we know of the "real world" is through our own thinking, and because everyone's thinking is different it could be said that every one of us lives in separate "worlds." In other words, one could say that the "real world" does not really exist for us except through our own thinking, and everyone's thinking is different.

It appears as if certain things that we take in through our senses tend to move our thoughts in certain directions and get the thought-feeling-behavior cycle rolling. In effect this is true because we then take those thoughts and run with them. The flaw is that the same event — or "trigger" — will cause different reactions in different people and even in the same person at different times. Some people may not have even registered something right in front of them that affected someone else very deeply. Thus, whether or not something exists as a trigger — something that prompts a thought or reaction — is only true as interpreted through our own thinking. In other words, we cause our own triggering (a humbling thought), which we then run with in different directions and at different speeds.

While we did want you to have this background in understanding, it will be interesting to try to get this across to students. Our advice is not to think about it. Let the curriculum do the work.

B. Key Points

◆ We can only experience what we perceive as "the real world" through our thinking.

◆ What appears to trigger us and set in motion the thought-feeling-behavior chain is really our own thinking.

◆ How we think determines what we feel and how we act, sometimes leading us in healthy, productive directions and other times into unhealthy, problem behaviors.

Sample Questions for Reflective Discussion

What do you think that a baby thinks when it comes into the world?

Why do you think your friends all act differently from each other?

What makes people see things differently, for example, how your parents see things differently than you do?

C. Needed Materials

Picture of little innocent cartoon baby.

Picture of cartoon baby with thought bubbles.

D. Opening Statement

[*If you used the Session Two "home practice" activity...*] For your home practice you were asked to think about and write down a behavior that you do in school or at home and what the thought-feeling-behavior links are.

ASK: What kinds of behaviors did you come up with?

[brief discussion]

ASK: Were you able to trace the links from your thoughts to your behaviors? What were they?

[brief discussion]

[If you used the alternate "home practice,"]

ASK: How many of you were able to notice your thoughts when you were at home? What did you notice?

[discussion]

In this session we're going to look a little more closely at how we pick up some of our thoughts.

E. Activity/Story Line

Have you ever wondered what we had on our minds when we were little babies and first came into this world?

Once upon a time — and this happens every day (in fact, it happens every second) — a baby is born.

You were one of those things once. Hard to believe, isn't it? Hard to imagine, isn't it? But it's true.

And when every little baby is born, have you ever wondered what they're born with? — what they bring into this world with them? — besides legs and gums and hair and spit and all that other stuff.

What's inside? (besides guts and blood and a heart and brain and all that.) What is in the baby's mind? Have you ever wondered?

Does a baby bring a bunch of problems into the world that s/he worries about?

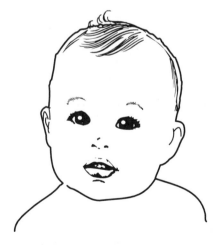

It sure doesn't look that way. When babies first come out they don't appear to have a care. It looks like they don't have anything on their minds except nice thoughts — like love, and dreamy peace, and wonder, and sleepiness, and ... "Wow, look at this place! What is this?" "I love this person who brought me here."

Of course they don't have words to think these things, but they still think.

And this was you, and this was me, and this was everyone! It happened to each of us.

So these are the kinds of thoughts we have UNTIL — and this happens almost immediately — the baby starts to take in the "world" through its thinking, like when the doctor or midwife smacks the kid on the bottom.

"OUCH!"

Or they get set down on a metal scale.

"HEY! THAT'S COLD!"

Or they start to get an uncomfortable feeling in their middle:

"THIS MUST MEAN I'M HUNGRY!"

Or they get an uncomfortable feeling on their bottom:

"OOOOH, HMMMM. WHAT'S THIS!? THIS MUST MEAN I'M WET."

ASK: Now, how can the baby get those things taken care of?

[entertain ideas]

"WHAAAAAAAA!!!!!" (crying)

ASK: When the baby cries, what do his parents do?

[entertain ideas]

Other people then miraculously respond or react.

"HEY, IT WORKED AGAIN!" "This is nice." "Hey, NOT SO ROUGH!"

So the baby learns what works to make him or her feel more comfortable, and what feels good and what feels bad.

Each baby starts to learn a way of seeing the world that this emerging person begins to carry with him or her.

The baby, of course, doesn't know any English or Spanish. But when she is dropped on a cold, hard table, something starts going on in her head that makes her think it's uncomfortable, so she starts crying. Even when we don't have words to express it, we still think thoughts of some kind that tell us whether something is warm or cold or soft or hard, or nice or bad, or anything. She may not have a language for it yet, but she thinks stuff like that just the same.

As we grow older, each one of us has different thoughts about whether things are warm or cool or anything else. For example, sometimes even in the same room, some people will be warm and others will be cold.

ASK: Why would this happen? Same room, some are warm, some are cold?

It's the same temperature. The only difference is our thoughts about it.

[Note: If someone says, "different metabolisms," ask how they would know what their metabolism was telling them?]

> How many of you have ever touched a worm? How about a snake? How many of you liked the way its skin felt? How about a cat's fur?

> How many of you like the taste of strawberries? How many like chocolate? How many of you like coffee, not coffee ice cream, but plain black coffee?

> How many of you really like rap music? How many are into heavy metal? How many of you like country music?

We touch things that feel yucky to us, such as a worm, but other people like the way it feels.

We taste things that taste wonderful to us, such as strawberries, but some people can't stand the taste of strawberries.

We hear things that sound great such as rap music and other people can't stand it.

We smell certain flowers and don't like the smell, yet our mothers have their noses buried in them.

We see people who we think are attractive, and others don't get turned on at all.

So, as we said in the last session, on the surface it looks like something is happening to us from "out there" that is causing us to feel a certain way through our senses, but really what we're responding to is our own thoughts about whatever we sense.

ASK: What do you think was going on in our heads when we were little kids and got scared because we thought a monster was under our bed?

[brief discussion]

Our thoughts were making us feel scared — triggering us to feel scared. Then we take those feelings and we run with them. It makes us do certain things. But we all react differently because we all have different thoughts about it.

ASK: Think of some things that make you worry.

Think of some things that stress you out.

Think of some things that bother you

Think of some things that make you depressed.

[List responses on the board in four different columns, one column for each item with a heading such as "worry," then take one column at a time and ask the above of each. Repeat for each column]

ASK: So where does the worry [the stress, the bother, the depression] come from?

[entertain ideas]

Everyone's own thoughts.

ASK: If you are worried about _____ [point to one of the items from the board] what might you then do? How might you act?

[entertain ideas]

What we do depends on how we think, since it can all be traced back to the first thought. The thought is what starts off the whole chain.

F. Home Practice

Notice the things that set you off, make you upset or angry or any other emotion. What does that thought make you then feel and do? Trace it back to where it comes from.

G. Summary

The only thing we can ever know about the world out there comes through our own thinking because we cannot experience anything except through our own thinking.

The entire chain—what we think, what we feel, what we do, and what we experience as a result is all set in motion by that one little thought or series of thoughts that sets it all in motion.

Ouch!
That's Cold?
I've got an intense feeling in my belly. This must be hunger!
I've got an intense feeling down there. I must be wet!
How can I get all of these things taken care of?
WAAAAAAAAAA!
Hey, it worked! I think I'll try that again!
"HEY, IT WORKED! "This is nice." "Hey, NOT SO ROUGH!"

Session Four

Sticky Thinking

A. To Teachers

Like breathing, thinking is the most natural process we engage in. Like breathing, we cannot stop. A steady stream of thoughts passes through us all day long. Not only do we think, but what we think affects every aspect of our experience.

Some of our thoughts are counterproductive and can take us away from feeling okay. Sometimes the thoughts we think get us stuck. We cannot seem to let go. The more we fight it, the more stuck we get. Alison Stickrod Gray calls this "sticky thinking." Sticky thinking can cause us to get mired down, to get in our own way, to bother other people, to cause harm. It may be useful to see what kinds of sticky thinking get in people's way. Until we see it, we can't do anything about it.

As the thinker of our thoughts we have the power to separate ourselves from any thought that makes us feel bad or confused or weak or uncomfortable. Probably the most important decision we can make is the choice about which thoughts to let go of and which to follow.

B. Key Points

◆ Some of our thoughts can bog us down and make us or others feel bad, such as "I can't do this" or "I'm dumb" or "He's stupid."

◆ When we see the "sticky thinking" that gets in our way, it puts us in a position to not get so caught up in it.

Sample Questions for Reflective Discussion

How do you tell which of your thoughts are good ideas to go forward with and which are bad ideas and best to drop?

How come when you're upset or angry or depressed about something, it seems hard to let it go? What makes it hard to let it go?

C. Needed Materials

The nonracist ("unbiased") version of the story of "Br'er Rabbit and The Wonderful Tar Baby," by Julius Lester [see condensed summary within this session].

About ten or fifteen cut-up "squares" of math paper for each student (about 4" x 4" or 3" x 5", whichever is easiest, large enough to write one short sentence on).

D. Opening Statement

In the last session we talked about what thought is. In this session we're going to talk about a certain kind of thinking that gets in our way and can make us or others feel pretty bad. This kind of thinking could be called "sticky thinking."

Suppose we have a problem that we feel bad about. Sticky thinking takes that problem and tries to stick it onto something or someone else.

For example, let's say we really want to hang out downtown with our friends but our parents won't allow it. We're bummed out, but we really want to go. So we try to figure out some way that we can possibly get to hang out anyway.

We might say to our parents, "I've got a school project I have to do with my friend." The thinking that preceded that statement would be an example of sticky thinking.

We might have thought to ourselves, "I really want to hang out, how can I do it? I know! If I tell them I'm doing something for school, maybe I can get away with going."

Here's what happened: We felt bad that we couldn't hang out, and we had a thought that allowed us to stick the problem onto something else; in this case, a lie. We thought this would make everything okay — until we learned that our parents called our friend's parents or the school, or they happened to be driving by and spotted us hanging out. Now we have another problem: we are also caught in a lie. And even if we are not caught, even though it may make us feel good to get away with something so we can hang out, deep down inside we probably feel bad that we had to lie to our parents. So trying to stick our problem onto the lie doesn't really work, because we still end up feeling a little bad, no matter what happens. And even if we think we don't feel bad, we probably still do, way deep inside.

See, inside we're really too smart to let ourselves be fooled by our own sticky thinking. It's impossible to fool ourselves. If we try to, something will come back on us, one way or another.

Sticky thinking only postpones having to deal with our problems. Then, when we finally do have to deal with them, we not only have our original problem to deal with, but we now also have additional problems to deal with caused by our sticky thinking. So even though it looks as if this kind of thinking helps at the time; in the long run it just makes things worse.

E. Activity/Story Line

[The teacher reads or shows or ad libs the nonracist version of the story of "The Wonderful Tar Baby" by Julius Lester. Here is a condensed summary]:

Frustrated that he wasn't able to catch Br'er Rabbit, one day Br'er Fox had an idea. He got some tar and mixed it with turpentine and shaped it into what he called a tar baby, and set him along the side of the road. Br'er Rabbit came bouncing along, sassy as all get out, until he spied the tar baby. Br'er Rabbit said, "Good morning" to the tar baby. "Nice weather we're having," but the tar-baby just sat there and didn't say a word. Meanwhile Br'er Fox lay low, hiding in the bushes. Br'er Rabbit said to the tar-baby, "Are you deaf, because if you are I can holler louder." When the tar baby still didn't respond, Br'er Rabbit said, "You must be stuck up then, and I'm going to teach you how to talk respectably to folks. If you don't take off that hat and tell me 'Howdy,' I'm going to bust you one." The tar-baby stayed still and didn't say a word. Br'er Rabbit kept asking him until he clenched his fist and punched the tar baby upside the head. His fist stuck and he couldn't pull it loose. Br'er Fox lay low. Br'er Rabbit said, "If you don't let me loose I'll knock you again." So he swung with his other fist, and that got stuck too. He said, "If you don't turn me loose I'll kick the stuffing out of you," and he kicked his foot and got stuck. Then he kicked with his other foot and that got stuck too. Br'er Fox still lay low. Br'er Rabbit squealed that if he didn't turn him loose he would butt him a good one. He butted and his head got stuck. Br'er Fox came out and said, "Howdy, Br'er Rabbit, you look sort of stuck up this morning," then he rolled on the ground laughing until he couldn't laugh any more. Br'er Rabbit was finally captured.

ASK: What kinds of thoughts did Br'er Rabbit have that made him get stuck?

[brief discussion]

ASK: What did those thoughts do to him?

[brief discussion]

ASK: Who made up those thoughts?

[brief discussion]

Here is a true story:

A high school basketball player was practicing basketball alone on a playground one evening as it was starting to get dark. He kept trying to dunk the ball through the hoop, but he kept barely missing. It frustrated him. He decided to go home, but before he did, he tried one more time to dunk the ball. Bang, again the ball clanked off the front of the rim, and he fell onto his back on the court. He got so mad and frustrated that he jumped up and grabbed hold of the rim. He kicked his foot up. It got stuck in the net. He couldn't get it free. He hung up there, holding the rim, with one foot stuck in the net. Now he was even more frustrated. So to try to get unstuck, he kicked his other foot up to kick it loose. That foot got stuck too. Now he was really stuck. Hanging up there up in the air he couldn't get loose. No one was around. His arms began to get tired. He started to panic. For ten minutes he hung up there. Finally he was afraid he wouldn't be able to hang on any longer and with a huge yank he ripped the net and his feet came out and he fell to the ground, nearly hurting himself badly.

ASK: What happened to this guy? What did his thinking do to him?

[discussion]

[Note: The following will probably come out in the discussion. If not, reinforce the point]:

The guy was upset that he couldn't dunk the ball. It felt a little bit better to get angry — at first. So with his anger he grabbed the rim and kicked, and got stuck. That anger was a sticky thought. He got more frustrated (another sticky thought) and kicked some more. Then he was really stuck. That's what sticky thoughts do to us: they get us in deeper.

ASK: What do you think Br'er Rabbit wished he had done instead? What do you think the basketball player wished he had done instead?

[discussion]

They probably wished that they didn't follow their thinking when they were frustrated and angry. When we cool down we have cooler thoughts that don't get us in deeper, but we'll talk more about that in other sessions.

For now we'll talk about those thoughts that get us in deeper.

Let's say your parents get mad at you for getting in trouble at school and they won't let you go to a party with your friends, as you had planned. You really wanted to go. It hurts.

ASK: What are some things you might think to yourself to take away the pain of not going?

[list on board]

[Note: Give the students enough time to respond. At first it may be difficult for them to come up with something. If no one comes up with anything, ask, "How many of you have ever been in this situation? If not with a party, then with something else your parents wouldn't let you do? How did you handle it? Did you say anything to yourself so you wouldn't feel so bad about it?" If they still cannot come up with anything, you may offer an example or two, such as: "Hasn't anyone ever said to themselves, 'I don't care about going anyway.' Has anyone ever said; 'It's her (or his) fault that I got in trouble.' What are some other things you've said to yourself?" Try to have the students come up with at least five things that they could say to themselves to stick the pain somewhere else, and list them on the board. Thus, you are ending up with five or more items on the board.]

[Point to one item on the list.]

ASK: If you said this to yourself, what would that do for you?

[entertain ideas]

For example, "I don't care about the party anyway." At first it seems to make you feel better. The flaw is, suppose deep down inside you really did care about the party. Then you still feel bad that you couldn't go, and now you also might feel kind of lousy that you're not really being honest with yourself. You've tried to stick your feeling on not caring, but it doesn't work.

[do this for each item on the list]

"I just won't tell them the truth." Again, we might be able to get away with it for awhile, but we might get caught and even if we don't we feel a little bad.

"It's her fault I got in trouble so I can't go." Again, deep down inside, you're the one who really knows whether it was someone else's fault or not. Even if someone else did do something to you to provoke you, you know that you're really the one who chose to act as you did.

Those are just some examples.

[The teacher should now place a letter in front of each item on the list on the board: "a", "b", "c", "d", "e." Now hand out to each student about ten or so "squares" of math paper.]

ASK: Look at the board to the first thing on our list. Now, take one of the squares of paper and write the letter "a." Now, individually, without putting your name on the paper, I want you to rate, on a scale from 1 to 5 (5 being the highest), how much you personally have a tendency to think in this way. In other words, when you feel bad about something or can't get your way, if you have the tendency to almost always say to yourself, (example) "Oh, I don't care anyway," you'd rate yourself a "5" on that item. If you never do it, rate yourself a "1." Then do it with the rest of the items on the list. Now, it's important to be honest with yourself here. Remember, all I want to see on the paper is the letter of the item, and your rating number. No names! Write that number down. Turn the paper squares over so the number isn't showing, and hand them in.

[For each item the teacher counts the ratings for each (or, better, have some students volunteer to count them), and writes the range of rating numbers on the board next to each item. We're not looking for an average, we're looking for the range. So it might look like "a: 1-4", or, if you have a small class you can write all the numbers.]

ASK: Now, this may have made you think of some other things that you have a tendency to say to yourself instead of what is up on the board. On another square of paper, write one thing that is not up on the board that you tend to say to yourself.

[Collect those sheets, shuffle them, and read them.]

ASK: Do any of these sound familiar?

We all have a tendency to think different things, in our own way, to try to scramble out of uncomfortable situations.

ASK: How would you sum up how "sticky thinking" might affect you? What does it do for you in the short run, and in the long run?

[discussion]

F. Home Practice

Count the times during the day that you are tempted to get into sticky thinking.

G. Summary

The whole point of sticky thinking is to make you feel better temporarily. There is one catch: later, you suffer the consequences of that sticky thinking on top of the original problem. This kind of thinking doesn't really do anything to solve the original problem. It only fools us into thinking that it's doing something to help us with that problem. Really, it only gets us in deeper, like Br'er Rabbit punching the tar baby in the face. It felt good at the time, then he realized he was even more stuck. The same with the basketball player; it make him feel better momentarily to kick out of anger, but then he was stuck, and he ended up feeling a whole lot worse.

Session Five

The Different Ways We Think

A. To Teachers

In the previous session we considered what a certain kind of thinking does to us. In this chapter we will delve deeper into the nature of "thought."

Most of us do not realize that we seem to have two separate and distinct thinking processes operating within us, or at least two different ways we use our thinking.

One mode of thinking functions like a computer and processes information. We fill our heads with information, draw upon memory, analyze that information, and we run programs. Some of the programs we run we know we're running, such as how to teach a math assignment, and other programs we run we have no idea that we're running, such as the way we tend to react if our spouse or partner does something that bugs us.

Our other mode of thinking functions more like a radio receiver, receiving free-flowing thoughts; that is, when the channel is clear it picks up signals. In this type of thinking we clear our heads, quiet our minds, and thoughts seem to pop up from out of the blue. Here, our thoughts just seem to flow freely; we are more receptive.

Deep inside, all of us are perfect, healthy beings. From our free-flowing thinking, out of a quiet mind, we sometimes have thoughts that surprise us. We might have insights. That's because this flow of thinking receives, picks up, taps into thoughts of wisdom and common sense. When our minds are clear we can hear this wisdom. All of us have had the experience of being in the shower or driving or walking or not thinking about anything in particular and, all of a sudden, having something pop into our heads, reminding us of something we've forgotten or giving us a new perspective on a problem. This is an example of how our health is always available to help us. All we have to do is learn to listen to it and pay attention to it.

B. Key Points

◆ The more we understand the difference between processing, computer-type thinking and free-flowing, clear-headed, receiver-type thinking, and when to use each, the more we will use healthy thinking to guide us.

◆ Receiver-type thinking connects us to our inner wisdom or common sense and to a natural, healthy free-flowing thought process.

Sample Questions for Reflective Discussion

Where are you or what are you doing when you get your best ideas?

What does this tell you about what you want to be doing with your mind to have the wisest thoughts, and give you answers to your problems?

Does a computer come up with new ideas? Can it? Why or why not? What about the computer in your mind?

What would you say is the pathway to your own wisdom, your own wise thoughts?

C. Needed Materials

None

D. Opening Statement

For your home practice last session, you were asked to count the times during the day that you are tempted to get into sticky thinking.

ASK: What did you find out?

[brief discussion]

We all do sticky thinking at times. There's no judgment about it. The only question is whether we want to follow that thinking.

Here is another surprise! We don't just think. We think in two completely different and separate ways.

ASK: Can you think of what these two different types of thinking might be?

[entertain ideas]

Don't worry if you can't come up with an answer. Very few people know about this. It is one of the best kept secrets in the world.

Here is a story to help you understand it.

E. Activity/Story Line

Once upon a time in the hilly regions of Brainville lived a person named Mr. [or Ms.] Slick Computerthoughts. Every day he would awaken from another night's sleep to face his rival in The Big Showdown.

The Big Showdown was a battle for who would win control of the precious jewel of the mind.

The stakes were high, for the battle took place at every moment the gladiators were awake.

Mr. Slick Computerthoughts, called "Slick" for short, was a master at making the mind think what he wanted. Slick would do whatever he needed to do, even be nasty and mean if he had to, in order to win the battle. He would lie, he would manipulate, he would use every trick in the book to win the mind-jewel. And he was good at it — an expert, the best at what he did. He was so good that everyone else ran for cover and hid.

When Slick felt good, he was an important guy to have around. He would help the mind figure out math problems, memorize facts, analyze how things fit together. No one could do it better.

But when Slick felt low and mean, he would make the mind do things such as punch people in the face, or cheat on a test, or be grouchy, or be worried, or be depressed, or get scared, or talk behind people's backs, or hurt people, or shoplift, or be filled with anxiety, or be promiscuous, or abuse others — physically, sexually, or emotionally.

Slick knew what he had to do to win the mind-jewel. All he had to do was to keep the mind filled and busy. He would throw in all kinds of information, all kinds of busy memories, both the good and the painful. Slick knew that as long as he kept the mind filled and occupied trying to figure things out, nobody else, not even his arch rival, would have a prayer of winning the mind. The more he made the mind grind away, the more the mind-jewel belonged to him.

Slick always knew that to win he had to be relentless. He could never give up. He had to be slick, so people wouldn't notice what he was doing to them. The more he made it all seem like the natural way to be, nobody would notice. So continually he tried to sneak around trying to slide things by. As long as he kept it up, nobody could get in his way. As long as he was in control of the mind — for that's what the mind-jewel was — the control would be his.

Yet none of Slick's bravado or sneaking around bothered his very formidable opponent: Mr. Cool Receiverthoughts.

Mr. [or Ms.] Cool Receiverthoughts — everybody called him "Cool" for short — lived in the deepest crevices of the brain. A completely different kind of fighter than Slick, he would spend his time hiding in his den and simply wait for Slick to let down his guard. Cool was cool — the coolest — and he was very wise.

Cool didn't even worry about winning the battle of the mind-jewel. Nothing bothered him, for he knew that all he had to do to win was to lay low and wait while Slick did his thing. Slick worked very hard to stay on top, but because what he did took a lot of energy, he would eventually get tired and would need to take a break. At that moment, Cool would strike with such precise quickness, that Slick wouldn't know what hit him.

Cool knew better than to mess with Slick when Slick was cranking away. At those times he knew he was no match for Slick.

No matter! In the showdown for the mind-jewel, Cool knew that all he had to do was wait.

Slick, on the other hand, knew he had to stay alert, or Cool would take advantage of even the slightest opportunity and defeat him.

Mr. Slick Computerthoughts didn't want Mr. Cool Receiverthoughts around. He tried everything he knew to keep him down, to keep him in his place, to keep him away. Sometimes, to keep him down, Slick would barrage him with all kinds of thoughts. Thoughts upon thoughts upon thoughts upon thoughts. When Slick was on top of his game, the thoughts came so fast and furious, it was like he was jumping on top of Cool's head.

But Cool was too cool to let Slick faze him. He would simply put up his steel umbrella and let the umbrella take the beating instead of him. So he could never be harmed.

Cool would hang in there coolly and wait. He knew that all he had to do was wait out Slick for a while. Slick would pound away and pound away, knowing he couldn't stop. If he did, even for a second, Cool would zip in and take over.

When Slick was on top of his game, Cool knew there was no sense fighting. Cool simply knew that he was tougher and smarter and funnier, and he didn't have to prove it to anyone. So Cool would just sit there, under his steel umbrella, weathering the storm, softly and beautifully playing his acoustic guitar.

Slick would pull out his heavy metal band to drown out Cool. Slick wanted the mind to listen only to him! Slick got a little jealous at times. But it wouldn't bother Cool. He would keep on playing. He knew that his acoustic guitar could not be heard when Slick's band was playing, drowning him out. But he also knew that Slick's band couldn't keep up the pace. At some point Slick and his band would get tired and have to take a break in the set. As hard as they tried, they just couldn't keep it up. And as soon as they took that needed break, even if they stopped for only a moment, Cool could be heard again playing so soft and so beautiful in the background.

Cool had the fortitude to never stop playing. He knew that no one could hear him most of the time because of Slick's loud band. He knew that when Slick stopped for that instant — even a second — Cool could be heard loud and clear, and that meant he had grabbed the mind-jewel. Cool always knew that Slick had to eventually stop for a rest because it was such hard work to keep trying to play so loud.

To hear Cool, all anyone has to do at any time is to get quiet. Then they hear him playing — in the form of wise thoughts that pop into their heads. This was Cool's main weapon: pop-up thoughts. Pop-up thoughts often deliver answers to questions, reminders that are helpful, creative, great ideas. This is the secret of the mind-jewel.

Often, Slick Computerthoughts and his band are so loud and powerful that we forget Cool Receiverthoughts exists. Sometimes when we don't hear Cool for a long time, we think he lost the battle and moved away, or is dead and buried somewhere. But that can never happen to Cool. He's too cool to be destroyed. He just talks so quietly, we often forget.

Sometimes when Cool catches Slick napping, Cool jumps through so quickly it's as if it happens automatically. He's so cool, he does it whenever he finds a moment of quiet. All of a sudden we get a thought from "out of the blue." We think: "Wow, where did that thought come from?" If we can't remember something or we forget where we put something and are trying really hard to remember it and we can't, then we forget about it, it may pop into our heads. That's Mr. Cool at work. Cool just smiles. He knows his thoughts can poke through whenever Slick shuts down the noise. Slick is tough, but he gets exhausted trying to keep up. He puts up a good fight, but it's tough work to keep it up all the time. No matter how good he is, he can't keep it up 100 percent.

Cool is so soft and quiet sometimes that if we don't pay close attention we may miss him. Slick tells us a lot of things. We listen to him. We may even like listening to Heavy Metal. Slick makes us feel a lot of stuff because of what he tells us. Slick makes us behave a lot in the way we do because of what he tells us. We tend to listen because his voice is louder. Slick's thoughts are familiar a lot of the time. We've heard them before. They sound like old familiar tunes. Cool's thoughts are often a surprise, because they jump out when we least expect it.

Of course there really is no Slick and Cool in our heads. It's our own thinking — two ways we use our own minds — and they're battling it our all the time. Here's what this means for our own lives:

ASK: Where are you or what are you doing when you get your best ideas?

[entertain ideas]

[Note: Odds are that the students will bring up things that they're doing when their mind is relaxed, when they don't appear to be thinking about anything in particular.]

It's always when our mind is quiet or relaxed or clear.

When a wise thought pops into our head from out of the blue, it's like Cool talking to us. The way it works is, we relax our processing, grinding away thinking, and we receive the pop-up thoughts.

In this way our mind works like a radio receiver. If the channel is clear we can pick up wise signals (from Cool Receiverthougths).

The other way we use our mind is more like a computer (Slick Computerthoughts). Slick loads our head with information and we process it. We draw upon our memory. We run programs. Without Slick we couldn't do math problems—at times like that we want Slick to win—but it's not so good for trying to solve our personal problems because we don't know all there is to know when we have a problem. We need fresh, new ideas at those times, fresh thinking, new insights. Only Cool can provide these. But when Slick is grinding away, it's like we get static through our receiver and we can't pick up the signals. Or, it's like mud on the windshield of a car. We can't see through it clearly.

By the way, this is one thing that young people can usually do much better than adults. Adults often have their heads too full; too busy. Slick takes over far too often.

ASK: So, we can hear Slick any time because he's always making noise and talking to us. But what do we have to do to hear Cool?

[entertain ideas]

The answer is to get quiet. Quiet the mind. Slow down our minds. Do something nice for ourselves where we forget about things. Calm down. Clear our heads.

When that happens, automatically we get Cool, wise thoughts.

If we know this, it means we get to decide who we want to listen to at any given time: Slick or Cool.

ASK: Think about a time when you can remember hearing wise, clear thoughts. What were you doing or what was happening? Pair up or get into groups of three and talk about it.

[Give the groups about 5-10 minutes to talk among themselves.]

ASK: So, what do you think is the moral of this story? What is the meaning of the precious mind-jewel?

[discussion]

The mind-jewel means which part of our thinking we allow to control our mind at any moment. The special beauty of it is that we get to create it anew at every moment with the power of our own thinking. At one moment we have Slick thoughts that we process in our heads; at another moment we have Cool thoughts that pop up in us. Our power is that we get to decide which to pay attention to. We get to decide which to give control to. We get to decide which thoughts we want to take to heart at any given time. And at every new moment it can change. We're never stuck with what we think. In the next moment we can think something else. Therefore we are continually creating our lives anew at every new moment with every new thought we think. There's new hope in every new moment.

Is that an awesome power, or what?!

F. Home Practice

See how many times this week you quiet down or relax your mind. Don't expect anything to happen. Just notice it as much as possible.

See if anything pops into your mind this week from out of the blue and take note of it. Notice what you're doing when it does.

G. Summary

Ideally, the students will say to themselves: "Wow, I never realized I have two different types of thinking in me that are always trying to get my attention. But I have the power in me to quiet my mind so I can listen to and be guided when needed by wise pop-up thoughts instead of unwanted, computer-process-type thoughts. I'm never stuck with the thinking I have. In a new moment I can have a new thought!"

Session Six

Feelings And Emotions

A. To Teachers

We have a built-in system for telling us if our thinking is on track: how we feel. If we're feeling okay inside (without having to depend on anything else for our happiness), we know that we're headed in the right direction. We could call these "noncontingent positive feelings," or, feeling good for no particular reason.

If we are feeling bad, or if we need some kind of stimulation from the outside to maintain our happiness, that signal means that we would be wise to alter our thoughts, or at least not take them seriously. Changing our minds is possible, especially when we know it is in our best interests.

Unfortunately, the deeper we get into the morass of lousy or negative feelings, the more seductive our thinking becomes. Yet, by understanding how our thinking works to create our emotions, we can save ourselves a lot of unnecessary heartache.

One of us heard from a client that a terrible thing had happened to her. She wanted to adopt a child and was in process of negotiating with an adoption agency. Unfortunately, the case worker with whom she was working took off with the agency's money and ran away, and the adoption agency was forced to close its doors. The client became terribly upset and discouraged thinking that she would never be able to adopt a child. For a long time she worried about what had happened. Eventually, one day the case worker returned the money. The agency reopened. The adoption proceeded. It suddenly occurred to the client what a waste of time and energy it had been to fret over something that worked itself out in the end anyway. She had been driving herself crazy with worried thinking, and she didn't need to. Whether she worried herself sick or not, whatever was going to happen would happen either way. If she had thought, "Oh well, whatever happens, happens," she would have had different feelings.

Besides, as Mark Twain once said, "I've had many worries in my life, most of which have never happened."

How often has a similar situation happened to you where you worried and worried and then whatever you worried about didn't happen? Worry and concern never solve anything. Yet when we're in the middle of worrying we can find any number of reasons to fret. This is called "self-validating thinking." When we understand how this works, we don't take our worries so seriously.

Here we need to make a distinction between emotions and feelings. Emotions such as fear, anxiety, anger, jealousy, blame, insecurity, and so on, are created by computer-process thoughts. Deeper feelings appear when we aren't burdened with heavy thoughts. Feelings such as joy, gratitude, love, humility, compassion, and humor automatically appear from free-flowing thought when we are touched by life, usually when we're not aware that we are thinking anything in particular, when our heads are clear.

B. Key Points

◆ We can tell how close we are to the health inside us by how we feel.

◆ If we're feeling some unwanted emotion, or need some kind of stimulation from the outside to maintain our happiness, the feeling is a signal that we're headed in the wrong direction.

◆ When we're feeling bad or even overly excited, we need to be open to the possibility that our thoughts may be giving us faulty information. In other words, things may not be as they appear at those times.

◆ When our heads are clear of any particular thoughts, we are more open to being touched by life and deeper feelings such as love, gratitude, joy, humor, compassion, humility.

Sample Questions for Reflective Discussion

How do you think you can tell whether you're heading toward your health and wisdom and when you're heading away from it?

What would our lives be like if we always saw traffic lights in our mind's eye that told us when to go ahead, when to stop doing what we're doing, and when to slow down and proceed with caution? What would that do for our lives? Do you think we have such signals built into us? What do you think they are?

C. Needed Materials

paper and pen or pencil

D. Opening Statement

ASK: For the last session's home practice, how many of you were able to quiet down your mind when you needed or wanted to? Raise your hands. How many weren't?

[Note: If some students were unable to clear their heads or quiet their minds, say something like, "That's not surprising. Most of us are just not used to doing it. We're out of practice. The more we are aware of it, though, the easier it gets."]

ASK: Did anyone get any cool pop-up thoughts they'd like to share?

[Hear from students but don't dwell on any of them. Simply acknowledge them with a "great!" or "Thanks" and move on.]

It feels nice to get those kinds of thoughts, doesn't it?

[Note: If someone says something like, "I got the thought that I'd like to kill my little sister," ask, "Have you ever had thoughts before that were similar? How often?" Depending on the answers and your evaluation of whether this thought is a message of annoyance expressed in hyperbole or serious consideration of violence, consider referring this student or any other student voicing violent thoughts to a counselor. If it seems like annoyance, then say something like, "If the thoughts are familiar, that is really Slick talking to us. Cool's thoughts are always fresh and new to us. But Slick is so slick, it's easy to be tricked."]

Okay. So far in this curriculum we have been talking about thoughts and thinking. Now it is time to talk about feelings.

ASK: How many of you have ever ridden in a car or bus or a four-wheel-drive vehicle?"

[show of hands]

ASK: What happens when you hit a nice big mud puddle, or a bigger truck goes by on a really rainy day or when it's all slushy in the road?

[entertain ideas]

All that slush and mud squirts up and covers the windshield. It's kind of hard to see out when that happens.

ASK: Then what usually happens?

[entertain ideas]

There's a switch or lever, maybe on the dashboard, maybe on the steering column to turn on the windshield wipers. Tah-dah, you can see clearly again.

Imagine you had a windshield wiper switch in your forehead. You're going along in life and something happens, you hit a big mud puddle, or a big truck comes by and squirts mud all over you. Your heavy thoughts are like that mud all over your windshield, preventing you from seeing out clearly.

ASK: What are some emotions you might feel with a lot of heavy thoughts on your windshield?

[entertain ideas such as angry, worried, upset, frustrated, bothered, jealous, etc.]

Now imagine you flip the wiper switch on and your mind windshield clears.

ASK: What are some of the feelings you might receive with your mind windshield clear?

[entertain ideas such as nothing, nice, peaceful, sharp, happy, relieved]

Suppose you're heavy into thought. You're upset about something. All of a sudden you get caught off guard by a beautiful scene such as a sunset, or your favorite song comes on the radio.

ASK: What happens to your busy, heavy thoughts at that moment?

[entertain ideas ~ examples: "they shut off", or "I get different thoughts."]

Usually, our minds clear in an instant as we get absorbed by the beauty or the song.

These might be similar to the feelings we get when the windshield in our heads is clear. The worst distractions are gone and we are open to receive new energy and new, creative feelings and thoughts.

E. Activity/Story Line

Did you ever hear the story about the farmer who had a beautiful herd of horses? His neighbor came by one day to exclaim how lucky he was to have such a herd. The wise farmer shrugged.

The next day the herd escaped through the door of the corral that had been absentmindedly left open by the farmer's son. The neighbor came to say how sorry he was. Again the farmer shrugged.

The following day the son had rounded up the herd again but in doing so broke his arm. Again the neighbor stopped by to express his delight for the return of the herd and his regrets for the boy's broken arm. Again the farmer shrugged.

The following day soldiers arrived to claim the boy for the army. However, upon seeing the boy's broken arm, they left the boy behind. The farmer shrugged again.

The poor neighbor didn't know what to make of all this.

ASK: What do you think is the moral of this story?

[discussion]

The wise farmer knew that everything had a way of changing, and he wasn't about to let his emotions get carried away with every good and bad event that happened.

TASK: Make a list of all the feelings and emotions you've had in the last week, or at least today. Write them on your papers.

Now, on your papers, next to each item on the list, place an "e" next to all the emotions that seemed to be brought on by what was happening at the time.

ASK: Can you see any difference between the emotions with the "e" next to them and the other feelings without an "e"? What is the difference?

[entertain ideas]

Emotions (such as anger, fear, anxiety, jealousy) are the result of our thoughts about what is happening out there, or what is happening to us. Feelings (such as joy, gratitude, love) seem to automatically happen when we are touched by life, often when we're not thinking anything in particular, or when our heads are clear, or when we're just taking in the moment.

What we're calling emotions seem to show up more when we're thinking something about ourselves personally, and what we're calling deeper feelings seem to show up more when we're just taking in the world around us and not taking things personally.

In other words, emotions are brought to us courtesy of Slick, and deeper feelings are brought to us courtesy of Cool.

Feelings don't just happen. They are the result of our thinking, but the thoughts go by so fast we don't recognize them as thoughts. We just feel the effects of that thinking. And, depending on where the thinking is coming from, we get different feelings and emotions.

TASK: Take a pen and paper and write a short paragraph about something that happened to you that you felt terrible about. No one else will see this. It's only for you. Then write down one word or maybe a few words that describe what your emotions were about what happened.

[Give them 5 or 10 minutes to do this]

ASK: How many of you still feel now exactly the way you felt at the time that you just wrote about?

[raise hands]

ASK: What changed? Did your feelings get less intense over time?

[brief discussion]

ASK: What are the implications of knowing that the things you felt so strongly about then are not the same things (or at least not as strongly) as we feel now?

[discussion]

Thoughts change, and with them the feelings and emotions we have.

ASK: What can we do if we find ourselves holding on to those emotions so much that it's affecting our lives?

[discussion]

At the time something powerful happens to us, nearly everyone gets hit by emotions and feelings at the time. That's only natural. After the event or situation is over, though, if we keep thinking thoughts that give us those emotions over and over again we might want to question how good it is for us to keep doing that. If we were able to let go of those thoughts our feelings would change. Later sessions will help us see how we can let go.

[Note to teacher: In a later session we make the distinction between what we are saying here and denial — there is a huge difference! Here we are only interested in raising the issue as "food for thought," so it is best not to get hung up about it here.]

Our feelings and emotions tell us how close we are to our health at any given time. They tell us whether our thinking is on track. When thoughts, and the feelings or emotions that come with them, are flowing through us and we are not placing a lot of importance on them, we are closer to the health inside us. The more compelling our thoughts are and the more we want to hold on to our emotions and let them grip us and rule us, the further we are from our health at those moments.

Here is a little chart that may help us see this better. These are examples of thoughts we have that bring us further from or closer to our health:

Feelings And Emotions

Far from health	Close to health
"I hate him for being that way!"	"It's interesting that he can be that way."
"She is against me and I'll show her!"	"She must not understand me. I'll see how to explain myself better or I won't let it bother me."
"This has to be taken care of right NOW!"	"I trust that I'll know when to take care of it when the time is right."
"I don't want to do this homework. I'll put it off."	"I don't feel like doing this homework but I know that if I take care of it then I'll be free to do what I want."

If we look closely we can see that a different feeling or emotion would be directly connected to the thinking we have about it. All day long we can tell ourselves things like this, on either side, but the feeling or emotion we get — if we pay attention to it — is what lets us know whether or not we are on the track of our health.

Feelings and emotions are signals, like traffic lights and road signs. If we feel emotions strongly and they are driving us to feel horrible, or to do stuff that's not good for us or others, if we are able to notice what we are feeling at the moment, it's like we get a red light that tells us: "Stop, you're headed in the wrong direction!" If we wanted to, we could then decide to listen to it and change course.

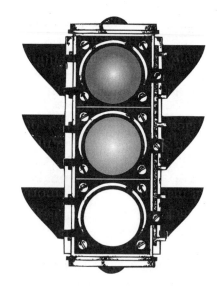

If we're feeling slightly yucky we'll get a yellow light: "Whoa, slow down, this probably won't lead you where you want to go." We could let that thinking go, or if we can't, just do something that makes us feel better so our minds are not focused on those other thoughts.

If we're feeling warm, or loving, or joyful, or we're happy, or feeling inspired, and it *doesn't* seem to depend on anything that we have to be doing to make us keep feeling that way [such as drugs or alcohol, or beating on someone, or bungee-jumping] — the green light says: "Keep going, you're on the right track!"

F. Home Practice

During the next week [or whenever], watch your feelings and emotions. See where they're coming from. See them as signals and see what happens. Notice when you continue to think about something after it is over, and what feelings and emotions you carry around as a result.

G. Summary

Circumstances and situations happen to us in life. We get feelings and emotions about them. But we've already learned that it is not the events of life that affect us, it is what we think about these events. What we think about often creates upset, anger, worry, blame. We sometimes let ourselves carry this emotional thinking around with us like heavy baggage, long after the event is over or the circumstances have gone away. If we continue to think about these circumstances and events, we might find ourselves living lives of upset, sadness, anger, fear, etc. Or, if we keep our minds clear and pay attention to the emotions and feelings as signals, and make adjustments when things don't feel right, we are more open to deeper feelings of enjoyment and satisfaction. Remember the chart of thoughts that indicate whether we're far from or close to our health.

Session Seven

Creating Our Behaviors: The Behavior Cycle

A. To Teachers

In the last session we looked at feelings. A close look at behaviors shows us that they are the result of feelings. For example, when people have loving feelings they behave in loving ways. When people have insecure feelings, they act it out in some way, such as disrupting a classroom or not participating in class. Loving feelings are preceded by loving thoughts; insecure feelings are preceded by insecure thoughts. These links on the chain — thought to feeling to behavior — can often form a cycle that spirals into what some might call a pattern of behavior.

We can observe these behavior patterns in people (and others can observe them in us). When we get to know someone we can often see that she or he reacts to similar situations in fairly predictable ways. What we are seeing is a series of thought → feeling → behavior chains that have become linked together in a cycle. A cycle repeats itself automatically.

How do behavior cycles start?

Let's review what we've learned for a moment and then take it a step further. Most of us tend to think that a stimulus in the environment triggers our response. For example, if we see a sign for donuts while driving along a road, we might stop the car and go in to get a donut. It looks as if the sign for the donuts triggered us and made us stop. But, really, a stimulus (such as the sign) becomes a trigger for us only when it is accompanied by a triggering thought such as, "Oh wow, that looks good," which causes the feeling of being hungry or craving a donut, which leads to another thought about getting a donut, which causes the action or behavior of getting the donut. Many people seeing the same sign would not stop for a donut. Why? They do not have the thought that makes it happen. Sometimes we see the same sign and do not have the same thought or feeling of hunger. This may happen after we've just eaten dessert and we're full. Conversely, if we're already thinking thoughts of hunger, we're apt to notice all the eateries along the way to the exclusion of everything else.

So our own thoughts can be so powerful that they can set the behavior chain in motion, and sometimes the same type of thinking can happen often enough to form a habit of thinking which produces the same kinds of feelings and behaviors over and over again to form a behavior cycle.

While this is a common process within everyone, the same process happens in the extreme. We can see it vividly in the young students who killed their fellow students and teachers. Remember, the cycle always begins with a thought, in that case with some form of insecure thinking such as, "I'm worthless," or "I'm no good," or "No one cares about me," or "No one likes me," or "Everyone calls me names," or "She did me wrong!" The feelings that arise with this insecure thinking are feelings such as hopelessness, uselessness, hatefulness. At first the insecure person may withdraw or go the opposite route and look to fight, but the behavior will always be some form of reaction to the feeling that comes from the insecure thinking. The behavior is something they've come up with to give them some kind of relief from their feelings. Yet, just as in developing drug tolerance, if that behavior goes on long enough and doesn't produce enough relief, at some point that behavior is not going to work for them any longer, and it is likely that the behaviors will get more extreme, more outlandish so that some relief will occur. The more outlandish the behavior, the more other people's thinking is affected by it. This reaction inadvertently produces more alienation which, in turn, leads to further thoughts and feelings that propel the cycle ever downward, in this case to the extreme action of murdering innocent people.

These students had never learned to recognize their own destructive thoughts as the problem. They kept thinking the problem was outside themselves, so they tried to eradicate it. To make matters worse, early in the cycle no one appeared to recognize that the students' destructive thinking would lead them in this direction or in some other horrible one. They unfortunately did not intervene before the cycle became deadly serious. The beginning of the cycle itself is serious, because some thoughts are taken very seriously.

Another place to see this cycle in the extreme is in adults and adolescents who involve children in sexual touching. Their stimulus may be a picture of what they see as a pretty, young child. Most people seeing that picture would not have thoughts of desire for that child, but for whatever reasons a few certain people get a thought that makes them want to touch that child sexually. This leads to a feeling of craving that child or some other child. At first, the person may want to act on it, but doesn't. Instead, the person just fantasizes. If it continues over a long period of time their fantasizing may not satisfy them any more. Again like drug tolerance, over time they need more of a stimulus to achieve the same excited feelings. Their feelings might become powerfully driven by even more outlandish thoughts. A pattern may develop. Whenever they are thinking bored or restless thoughts, they may develop a habit of looking at child pornography, or they may aimlessly drive around looking for a victim, or they might now do whatever they need to do to satisfy this feeling. If the cycle progresses further it may lead to the behavior of a sexual offense against a child.

To break such a cycle, people must see the destructive pattern. They must step back and look at it instead of being caught up in it. The more they see the relationship between their thoughts and feelings and behaviors that propel the cycle, the better chance they have to catch the pattern early and stop it before it gets carried too far. The earlier they catch the destructive thinking and see it as such, the better off they and society will be. If they understood the mechanism and saw it at work they may, for example, catch themselves feeling an emptiness inside, and they might see themselves wanting to do something to try to fill that void. When they do try to fill that void by following through on their fantasy, they may be able to see that, at best, the relief is only temporary. When it is over they feel worse and have to do it again to continue to feel okay.

Less extreme, let's say someone is on a diet and their compelling feelings caused by their thinking just made them gobble down a dozen cookies. Like the sticky thinking, although they enjoy it at the time, when it is over they often feel guilty (they think guilty thoughts about themselves and experience the effects of it as feelings) and, thus, feel worse afterwards. Then those low thoughts may trigger another cycle that brings them even further down or leads them into even more extreme behaviors such as in bulimia or bingeing and purging.

Here is how a behavior cycle works:

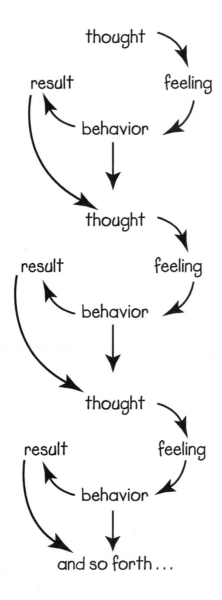

B. Key Points

◆ Some thought→feeling→behavior cycles lead to patterns that lead people down problem paths — for themselves and/or others.

◆ People who can observe that they are in a behavior cycle or pattern caused by their thinking are in a position to do something about it, and the earlier the observation the better.

Sample Questions for Reflective Discussion

How would you feel and act if the person you were dating went out with someone else without telling you? Everyone write down your answers (without using names), let's collect them, and I'll read them off, and we'll compare them.

What would make the different people in this room react so differently?

What would you think causes different people to behave differently?

C. Needed Materials

A blackboard or newsprint to write on, or an overhead projector and transparency of a behavior cycle [see end of session].

D. Opening Statement

ASK: In your home practice, were you able to watch your feelings and emotions as signals? What happened when you did watch them? Did they get stronger or get weaker?

[discussion]

Usually if we observe our emotions from a little distance, they get weaker. The reason they get weaker is because if we're looking at them from a step back, we're not caught up in them and then we can do something about them. [We'll come back to this later].

For now, consider this: have you ever wondered why your friends seem to act in the same kinds of ways over and over again?

For example, if a certain friend gets insecure, he'll almost always get angry and maybe try to hurt somebody. Another friend who gets insecure will almost always try to put somebody down. Another might act like a clown. Another might withdraw and not talk to anyone. Interesting, isn't it? Different people seem to act out the same kinds of behavior patterns over and over again.

ASK: Any ideas where these patterns come from?

[entertain ideas]

To understand this we have to remind ourselves again where behaviors come from. Remember the bicycle chain? Something happens out there, or we see something, and then we get a thought about it, and that thought leads to a feeling, and that feeling leads to a behavior.

E. Activity/Story Line

Suppose a guy has an agreement with his girlfriend to only date each other. But after a few weeks his girlfriend goes out to a movie with another guy without telling him.

ASK: What are some possible things the guy could think?

[On the board, list at least five possibilities]

Examples: "I'm going to get back at her!" "I'm so depressed!" "Oh, well, I'll find somebody else." "I'll never go out with another girl as long as I live." "How could she do that to me!?" "I'm not good enough."

ASK: Now, go back through the list [one at a time] and tell me what some possible feelings might be for each of those thoughts.

[write on board]

Examples: anger, sadness, resignation, excitement, disgust, disbelief, jealousy

ASK: Now go back through the list of feelings and suggest what some possible behaviors might be that might come from those feelings.

[write on board]

If the students have trouble coming up with things, here are a few possibilities.

If the thought is:	that may make him feel:	and it may lead him to:
"How could she do this to me?!"	angry	to put his fist through a wall
"I can't let her get away with this!"	revenge	to do something bad to her
"I'll teach him!"	revenge	to punch out the guy
"I'm not good enough."	insecure	to get depressed
"She made a mistake, must not have realized that would hurt me."	understanding	to talk with her
"Oh well, there are lots of other girls out there; I'll find someone else to take out."	okay	to find someone
I'm not going to let this bother me!"		

The thought you get about a situation leads you to feel a certain way, and the feeling you have makes you want to behave or act in a certain way.

Each of those behaviors or actions might produce a different response or a different result.

ASK: Now, go back through the list again and consider what might be a possible result of each behavior?

Again, if the students have trouble coming up with something, here are some examples:

Behavior	Result
put fist through wall	hand hurts property possibly damaged others get mad at you
do something bad to her	she doesn't want to have anything to do with him any more
punch the guy	get in trouble with the principal the kid pulls a knife or gun the kid's gang comes after him gets arrested for assault
get depressed	others feel sorry for him, or they consider him a wuss
talk with her reasonably	she might understand his feelings and feel bad about what she did and make it up to him, or he might find out that she really didn't care that much for him
take someone else out	he forgets about her and has a good time, or he realizes it isn't as much fun as with his girlfriend

There are lots of possibilities. The point is, different results are produced from different behaviors which come from different feelings which come from different thoughts. But each result produces another set of thoughts — its own set of thoughts — that causes another set of feelings, another set of behaviors, and another set of results, which would produce another set of thoughts, and so forth.

Sometimes people get into set patterns that repeat themselves because they get used to dealing that way. Here's how it works:

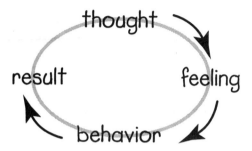

Let's say you did poorly on a test in school and a thought crawls into your head: "I'm dumb!" You don't know where the thought came from, but all of a sudden that thought is in your head. Here's what a lot of people do when they get a thought like that.

---

* Adapted from the work of Dr. Roger Mills.

This is how an innocent little thought can set off a chain of behavior that can become a pattern of thinking that spirals downward. When people respond in a similar way over and over again, the pattern then becomes a cycle.

People get used to acting in a certain way, and they don't really know why. If we don't know why it's happening, there's nothing we can do about it — because we can't see it. But if we start to see our patterns, then we're not so caught up in them — just like with seeing our feelings.

Sometimes it's easier to see the patterns in someone else than in ourselves.

If we see someone behaving in ways that we consider to be odd or bad, we might be able to see or surmise what might be the thoughts and feelings that might lie behind that person's behavior that might have led to their behavior pattern.

For example, even when people dress a certain way, they have gotten into a pattern or cycle of dressing that certain way.

ASK: What would make someone dress a particular way?

[discussion]

ASK: What would make someone knock over books in school to get a few laughs? or beat someone up? or get high? or sexually abuse others?

[discussion]

Here's where it gets tricky. We know that people get into habits of thinking and behavior without really being aware of them, and that this can lead to a downward spiral (as in the example with "I'm dumb."). If someone is in pain or feeling lost or feeling empty, they could really get onto a destructive course without knowing what they're doing. Because, whatever they're doing, it is just a way of relieving their pain — only they don't realize it.

People don't like to feel pain or to feel empty inside, so without knowing what they're doing they have all kinds of thoughts that help them to relieve the pain — only (as with "sticky thinking") it usually causes them more pain down the line.

TASK: Think of a kid you know, or that you see around school, or a parent, or a friend. What patterns of behavior do you see in that person? In other words, when something happens, how do they tend to react? Pair up with someone and, without using any names, and without being obvious, talk about what you see. What would you guess is the thinking behind that person's behavior?

[Give students about 5 or 10 minutes for this activity]

We're just like that, you know, with our own behavior patterns — only maybe not so extreme (or maybe more extreme, in some cases). But we can't see our patterns (just like they can't see theirs).

ASK: The question is, what can be done about it? Suppose we have gotten ourselves into a downward spiral or a destructive cycle, what can we do about it?

[discussion]

Just see it! See the pattern.

Remember, the entire pattern started with that first thought. Back to the "I'm dumb" example — that first thought came into the person's head, the person took it seriously and believed it, and everything — feelings and behaviors and more thoughts — took off from there and went out of control.

So what does that tell you about how not to let a pattern like this develop? Once you see it (realize it) it will be a lot harder to get behind it and follow it.

It all comes back to that first thought. In this example, "I'm dumb." The key is to know that we all get thoughts like this from time to time (particularly when we're in low moods), but thoughts like that don't mean anything. They're just crazy thoughts that just appear in our heads from time to time.

Once we see that thought, we have two choices: 1) we can either take it seriously, in other words, we can think we really are dumb; or, 2) we can not take it seriously and dismiss it.

We don't need to take these thoughts to heart. We can just let them go. We can say to ourselves, "Wow, that was a crazy thought. Whew!" and just let it go. When we let it go, we do not give it power over us. That is the great part! If we don't do anything with that thought, if we ignore it, the thought will naturally and effortlessly flow right out of our head — until it comes back again, and then we can let it go again, and if it comes back again we can let it go again, and again.

In later sessions we will see what to do if we've already gotten into a troubling pattern of behavior that we can't seem to control.

F. Home Practice

Think about a behavior that you seem to do a lot that maybe doesn't make you feel very good. See it as merely a pattern that developed from your way of thinking and the cycle it has caused. But don't dwell on your thinking about it. Don't try to figure it out. Just notice that it's there. If you see it for what it is, your awareness will begin to take the power away from it.

TASK: For the next class, everyone please bring in either your favorite story, or your favorite poem, or your favorite song.

G. Summary

The thing wrong with the way people act is that their thinking has triggered a pattern of behavior that they are probably unaware of. They get so used to it that it becomes the way they respond. It becomes a pattern. If a pattern leads us where we don't want to go, to break the cycle we need to see the pattern for what it is and realize that it initially came from a simple little innocent thought that we turned into a monster. Seeing it turns the monster back into simply a set of thoughts that only have the meaning we decide to give it.

Session Eight

The Different Ways We See The World

A. To Teachers

How we view the world comes from how we were brought up, the experiences we've had, and how we've come to think about those experiences. Since we all have different experiences and since the important people in our lives have told us different things, we could say that we each construct for ourselves a unique world view. Our distinct world view is what creates an Archie Bunker or a Pollyanna and everything in between.

Every day we make loads of decisions. The question is, on what are those decisions based? It should be no mystery by now that they are based on what we think — about ourselves, about others, about life.

In essence, every decision we make is based on our respective world views, because each view looks real to each of us — even though it is different for everyone. If we think the world is an unpleasant place with difficult people, it becomes our experience.

The more we recognize the true source of our decisions (our world view) as thought, the less our thoughts affect our behaviors.

Even when we're not aware of our thinking, when we realize that our feelings and behaviors are of a low quality, we're tipped off that we're doing some sort of low-quality thinking. But we'll come back to this last statement in a later session.

B. Key Points

◆ People acquire different world views depending on their unique sets of thoughts.

◆ Our view or perception of life changes with our thinking.

◆ The key is to not see our view as "the way it is," but as "the way we happen to be seeing it now, and that can change."

C. Needed Materials

a favorite book or short story

a painting on a postcard, greeting card, or art book

words to your favorite song

paper and pencil or pen

Sample Questions for Reflective Discussion

Does your life look different to you at different times, like, pretty good sometimes, and other times pretty bad? How can you tell which view is accurate?

What do you think it means that it's easier to change what's on our eyeballs than it is to change the way others behave?

When a person acts in a similar pattern about lots of different things, what do you think it means?

D. Opening Statement

Today, we're not going to begin with your home practice — unless someone has a really burning point that they'd like to make, or a burning question to ask.

[Give the group a few moments to respond, then move on]

Since we all live on the same planet and we are all born in pretty much the same way, have you ever wondered why it is that some people seem to enjoy themselves most of the time, and others seem to have such a hard time?

Is it luck? Is it fate? Why?

Why is it that two people who grew up in the same family could have such a different experience of life that one of them ends up an alcoholic and the other as President of the United States? [Billy and Jimmy Carter] Why is it that in some low-income families one kid will end up in jail and another as a university professor?

What's the secret?

The key to unlock this treasure chest, filled with pearls of wisdom, is found in this session. What if we each had the key to this treasure chest?

We do!

It is incredibly exciting to realize that we can unlock a life full of satisfaction and contentment. All we need is the key!

E. Activity/Story Line

Most people are under the mistaken illusion that our life unfolds from the outside-in. In other words, whatever situation we happen to find ourselves in is what we're stuck with.

ASK: Raise your hand if you have ever noticed that some adults see a lot of problems in their world and that others see a lot of opportunities. Do you have any examples of this?

[entertain ideas]

ASK: Raise your hand if you have ever noticed that some adults are creative and joyful, and others complain and regret a lot. Do you have any examples of this?

[entertain ideas]

ASK: What do you think is the difference between these people?

[discussion]

The difference is not what happens to these individuals, but their view of what happens — the way they see what happens to them.

Remember a few sessions ago we learned that whatever we take in through our senses mixes with our thoughts about it and becomes our experience? Then we get our own, special experience based on how our thinking takes in what we sense.

For example, have you ever seen a classmate walking down the hall with his usual "I'm cool" walk and talk, then a teacher walks by and says "Hi, what's up?" and he turns and angrily snaps, "Nothing!" then walks away shaking his head?

ASK: What do you imagine might be this kid's experience of life?

[entertain ideas]

On their journey through life, people can have a nearly infinite variety of experiences, depending upon what has happened to them and what they allow in. Some people miss out on golden opportunities, and other people carry beliefs with them that can place them in deadly situations.

Let's say a teenager truly looks up to one of his peers. The kid seems so cool. He seems to have it made, always getting away with things, living on the edge, and so forth. So the teen follows the kid's lead and winds up getting arrested for stealing. Suddenly he may start thinking differently about what he thinks is cool, or maybe he sees that a life of crime is now his life.

TASK: Think of anything in your life when at one time you viewed something one way and later, as you grew older, you saw things in a different way. What do you think changed?

**[Break up the class into small groups of about four to talk about it.
Give them approximately 10 minutes.]**

[Come back to the large class.]

ASK: After listening to everyone in your group, what conclusions can you draw about what makes the difference in changing someone's view?

[discussion]

[Note: At this point the astute student will likely say that the difference is thought, but see if you can get them to be more specific. What about thought changed, and what made the change happen?]

There really is no answer. We only know that people's view changes from within, but we have no idea what causes a change in someone's thinking. It just seems to happen. Sometimes experiences and situations seem to have something to do with it, and sometimes they don't. Sometimes age appears to have something to do with it, and sometimes it doesn't. The important point is that, no matter what causes the change, we all think that the way we are seeing things now is really the way it is, and then our view shifts somehow and then we think that new way is the way it really is, and then it shifts again and again over time. So what we think is real isn't necessarily so.

ASK: Does whether or not you have nice feelings change according to your world view?

[discussion]

If we want a nicer experience of life, the key is to understand that because our world views are so different from everyone else's, and because our world views keep shifting, nothing is carved in stone or fixed about the "world" we see. Nothing is fixed about the life we see. Nothing is fixed about who we see ourselves to be. Nothing is fixed about other people we see. Everything we see can change WITH THE VERY NEXT THOUGHT!!! So we get to decide how bummed out or angry we want to be now because of what we see — if we know that what we see now might change in the next moment with a new thought.

This is the key to the treasure chest!

ASK: Why do you think this is the key to the treasure chest? What do you think it means for you?

[extensive discussion]

It raises an interesting point. Instead of reacting to something out there in the world, if we know that something about the way we see it (think it) may change, how stuck do we want to be on what we're feeling about it now? Instead of trying to change something out there in the world we could first change our world view. We could change what comes in through our own eyeballs.

ASK: How do we do that? How can we change our view if we're stuck with our own view?

[entertain ideas]

Sometimes — often — it is not so easy to change what we see. The idea is not to TRY to see something differently. That is usually too hard. But if we look very closely we can see that what comes in through our own eyeballs does change from time to time. The same thing can look different to us at different times. The key is to not see our view as "the way it is." Instead, we want to see it as "the way we happen to be seeing it now, and that can change." The more we take a step back and see ourselves as the thinker of our own thoughts instead of being stuck with whatever we are feeling or experiencing, the better off we will be.

There are always possibilities other than the way we're seeing it now. We can realize that seeing it in a different way is possible with a different thought or a different set of thoughts, and that could happen at any time.

Something out there that we're seeing as difficult now, we might see as nicer later on. It can change. We get to decide if what we see is what we want, in the form of the feeling it gives us. If we think something out there in the world is fixed and it's depressing us, we're stuck with the feeling. If we think that same thing is fluid and changing, the feeling doesn't seem to get to us as much, or it doesn't last as long.

Another way to say this is that we can observe our own thinking and decide whether that thinking is doing good things to us or bad things to us. Our feelings will let us know which it is. If we don't know which it is, if we quiet our minds, our wisdom will tell us. Remember Mr. (or Ms.) Cool? If we're quiet enough to listen, we can hear what's best for us.

If we don't see a way out of a problem now, we will see a way out at another time — because we'll have different thoughts about it. For example, if our slick thoughts rule, we may be stuck in it, but if our mind calms or clears and our cool thoughts rule, we may see the way out.

There is something we can do! We can do whatever we can to clear our heads or slow down that stuck thinking. Then we'll see it differently, and we'll feel differently, and we'll probably act differently.

We'll explore some of the ways that it is possible to see things in later sessions. For now, all we have to know is that our world view can change — and it does — and it will.

This is the key to the treasure chest. This is the key to having a nice life.

This point may be difficult to understand. If you are having trouble understanding this now, don't worry about it. It will become more clear in the next session and throughout the rest of this curriculum. So, we will talk more in the next session and in future sessions about what this key means.

F. Home Practice

TASK: Here is your assignment. There are five parts.

1. Find your favorite story, or your favorite book, or your favorite poem or your favorite song.

2. Write a paragraph about what you think the world view is of the author, artist or composer.

3. Then, suppose that the author or composer had the opposite world view. How would the author, artist, or composer's work change with this new, opposite view? Write another paragraph about how you think the work would change — what it might look like. Or, rewrite the work or re-do the drawing from the perspective of the opposite world view.

4. Write a sentence about whether you think the work would still be your favorite if it was written with this different view, and why.

5. Write a sentence or paragraph considering whether it was the artist's or author's or composer's world view that attracted you in the first place?

The more time you take with this, the more you throw yourself into this, the more you'll get out of it.

[Note: Collect these at the beginning of the next session and begin the next session with a discussion of what, if anything, they learned from doing this exercise.]

G. Summary

We may not be able to do so much about the circumstances we find ourselves in or the events that happen to us in life. What we can do something about is the way we see those events and circumstances. The way we see things now isn't necessarily the way we will see them later. What we think is so right now, we may not think is so right later. Our world views can change — and they will. So how seriously will we take what we now think is right?

If we want a nicer experience of life, we want to point our thinking in that direction — or at least know that we can.

Session Nine

The Fork In The Road: Which Path Will We Go Down?

A. To Teachers

Up to now in this curriculum we have been dealing with what creates people's feelings and behaviors. We must now learn what to do when faced with unwanted feelings and behaviors.

As we walk along the road of life we are confronted with many situations, events, circumstances, feelings. At each such place, we find ourselves at a fork in the road. Whichever leg of the fork we choose to walk down will take us to a completely different place — to different feelings, different behaviors, and different results.

The purpose of this session is to help the students understand the fork in the road, and help them reflect on which path they may want to take, instead of blindly plowing ahead.

B. Key Points

◆ Every day we are faced with many different decisions that can lead us down a healthy path or a problem path, and each time we are faced with such a thought, we are at a fork in the road.

◆ The road we choose starts the cycle rolling either toward our health or away from it — either toward problems or away from them.

◆ We get to choose which prong of the fork we will walk down, and we get to experience the results or consequences of whatever decision we make.

◆ A new fork can appear at every new moment. We are never stuck on a particular road.

Sample Questions for Reflective Discussion

If you were walking through the woods and came to a fork in the road, and on one path it said, "to your health and wisdom" and on the other path it said "to problems, reactions, and misery" which one would you choose? What if you knew you were always at that fork at every moment in your lives? What would it mean for your life?

Do you think there might be one reliable way to go about making decisions each time you come to a fork in the road?

C. Needed Materials

Robert Frost's poem: "The Road Not Taken" (included within this session)

D. Opening Statement

ASK: What, if anything, did you learn from the assignment about your favorite author/composer/artist's world view, and if it changed?

[discussion]

This session will help clarify the key to the treasure chest from the last session.

[The teacher draws a fork in the road on the board.]

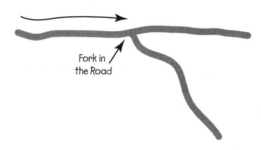

Fork in
the Road

Suppose you are walking down a path through the woods. All of a sudden the path splits in two. One of the paths goes right; the other goes left. This is called, "a fork in the road." There are no signs that tell you which path to take. What do you do? How do you know which path to take? Do you think anything might happen to you differently if you choose one path over the other?

That is what this session is about.

E. Activity/Story Line

I would like everyone to relax and take some deep breaths and close your eyes. I'm going to read you a poem, and I just want you to take it in quietly.

[Read Robert Frost's poem, "The Road Not Taken." (1916)]

Two roads diverged in a yellow wood,

And sorry that I could not travel both

And be one traveler, long I stood

And looked down one as far as I could

To where it bent in the undergrowth;

Then took the other, just as fair,

And having perhaps the better claim.

Because it was grassy and wanted wear;

Though as for that, the passing there

Had worn them really about the same;

And both that morning equally lay

In leaves no step had trodden back

Oh, I kept the first for another day!

Yet knowing how way leads on to way,

I doubted if I should ever come back.

I shall be telling this with a sigh

Somewhere ages and ages hence;

Two roads diverged in a wood, and I —

I took the one less traveled by,

And that has made all the difference.

Robert Frost

ASK: What does this poem mean to you — about your own life?

[Brief discussion. Every answer is right.]

Suppose you're walking down a road that in this case happens to be the hallway of your school. All of a sudden you get the urge to push a kid into his locker, or make fun of a boy coming toward you. Did you know that at that moment you are also at a fork in the road?

ASK: What do you think the two roads are that are ahead of you?

[brief discussion]

ASK: What do you think might happen if you take one of the roads compared to the other? What might be the different outcomes for each path?

[brief discussion]

It all can be traced back to that one point of decision, that one thought you had that you could have taken in one direction or another.

ASK: When you get a thought like that, how many of you stop, stand back and reflect for just a moment about the two different paths that lie ahead before acting?

Probably we all don't do that enough. But we could.

ASK: What do you think would happen if we did stop for a moment and reflect?

[discussion]

Now, here's something else. There's another fork in the road that we face all the time without knowing it:

Suppose we are walking down a road and all of a sudden we get hit with a feeling of insecurity (which we now know comes from a thought of insecurity).

Let's say you've been invited to a party and you see an attractive person of the opposite sex, and you think, "Wow, I would really like to meet him [or her]." But all of a sudden another thought comes into your head: "Maybe I'm not good looking enough. Maybe that person won't even pay attention to me."

ASK: Do you see a fork in the road? What fork do you see?

[simply entertain anyone's ideas without discussion]

Here's another situation. Your teacher calls on you in class, and you are unprepared to answer the question. The teacher then says, "I should have known. You're never prepared. You'll never amount to anything."

You suddenly get a feeling of extreme embarrassment and insecurity.

ASK: Does anyone see a fork in the road here? What would be the two different prongs of the fork in this case, in terms of what you might say to yourself about what you're feeling, given what the teacher did?

[entertain ideas]

On one path of the fork, you might say to yourself, "The teacher embarrassed me and made me feel insecure."

On the other path, you could say to yourself, "I'm feeling embarrassed and insecure because of my thinking."

This second path means, your teacher may have done something that a lot of people would consider wrong or inappropriate, but it is your own thinking about what the teacher did that made you feel embarrassed or insecure about it.

This has nothing to do with excusing the teacher's behavior. What the teacher did could be considered inappropriate or wrong. But what you do with it is how it affects YOU!

ASK: What might happen differently to your feelings if you took one fork compared to the other?

[brief discussion]

See, it is not wrong to feel embarrassed or insecure in a situation like that. That feeling is very real. But it is important to know where it is coming from — what the source of it is. This is all we are saying: realize the source — no value judgment about it, no right or wrong, no good or bad. Simply recognize the source. If you want to say that what the teacher did was wrong, fine! But the source of your feelings is always yourself, not other people or things.

The point of this is that two different things happen to us when we take one path of the fork or the other:

1) If we blame our feelings on the teacher, as long as the teacher is still in our face we are likely to get more and more insecure, or our insecurity will turn into being mad at the teacher, or something like that.

2) If we recognize that the real source of our feelings is our own thinking, just by recognizing it, we gain a little bit of distance from that feeling. In other words we are watching ourselves have the feeling, which feels different from being caught up in the feeling. In this case we are looking at ourselves having insecure thoughts or angry thoughts. That distance is like insulation in a house that protects us from the cold. That distance in looking at the source of our feelings protects us from being swept away by those feelings.

ASK: What questions do you have about this? Does this make sense? Tell me about what this means to you.

[discussion]

Now let's move back to the party, seeing that attractive person.

The fork in the road:

1) On one prong of the fork, I have this yucky feeling, "Oh God, maybe I'm not good looking enough," and I take it to heart. I believe it. Because I believe this feeling is being caused by my being in the presence of this beautiful creature, the longer he or she is there in my presence, the more my mind grinds away about whether I have the courage to talk to him or her. I then conclude that I don't have the courage because I'll get rejected because I'm not attractive enough, and I feel worse and worse as the party goes on.

2) On the other prong of the fork, I say (something like): "Wow, I just got this flash of insecurity about myself. Isn't it interesting that my own thinking would do that to me. It's just one of those crazy thoughts that we all get from time to time. It doesn't really mean anything."

As soon as we see the source of our feeling as our own thinking, it takes the power out of it. We don't feel worse and worse as the party goes on. Instead, the worst that happens is we remain neutral. Usually what happens is, separated from that feeling by a little insulation or distance, we begin to feel a little better and go on about our business. We may or may not decide to approach that other person, but whether or not we do we're not sitting around stewing over how bad we feel.

This is the difference made by recognizing the fork in the road in whatever situation we find ourselves facing.

In summary, down one fork we blame our feeling on the circumstances we are in or the situations happening to us out there. Down the other fork we take responsibility for the way we are feeling about the situation.

[point to the picture of the fork]

The first fork (the low road) spirals us toward feeling worse. The second fork (the high road) spirals us toward feeling a little better.

[draw spirals up and down at the end of each prong of the fork in the diagram]

Two roads diverge in a yellow wood. We get to choose.

By taking responsibility for our own feelings we are taking the one less traveled by, and that makes all the difference.

F. Home Practice

The next time you feel an emotion such as anger, or insecurity, or worry, or anxiety, or jealousy, or you get bothered by someone, or you feel any other emotion that you see yourself feeling, put yourself at the fork in the road, and decide which path you want to go down.

G. Summary

Each time we have an emotion, at that moment we are at a fork in the road. We can either take the high road or the low road. The low road is blaming our feelings on our circumstances. The high road is to say "I am feeling this way because of the way I am thinking." The low road spirals downward. The high road spirals upward.

Session Ten

Moods

A. To Teachers

Everyone has moods. We have them like the ocean has tides. They are like clouds passing in front of the sun. But we must remember that the sun is always still there. It doesn't go anywhere; it is only temporarily hidden from us.

Our thinking and our moods are directly linked. In a low mood we think low quality thoughts. In a high mood we think high quality thoughts. Depending on our moods, we can see the same situation completely differently, and it affects how we act.

Two important things about moods are: 1) if we are aware of them we can decide how we act when we're in them; 2) if we leave them alone, they pass. In a low mood, we need to be patient and let it naturally pass, which it will do eventually — guaranteed.

No one lives without moods. Sometimes it is hard to live with them. Moods happen all day long. Everyone goes up and down — some more than others and for varying amounts of time, but the process is the same for all human beings.

On the surface, it sometimes appears as if being tired or hungry triggers a low mood. On the surface, moods seem to follow external events; for instance it looks as if good news brings a good mood, and bad news brings a bad mood. However, all is not what it seems. Our well-being is not tied to any outside source such as an event or a circumstance. To know this is a relief. However, if we judge something as bad or wrong and think that our well-being is tied to it, then we are at the mercy of that outside "thing," and we suffer unnecessarily with a bad mood.

Most of us would prefer to be in a joyous, grateful mood, rather than be in a sullen, dejected mood. Yet, the authors of this curriculum prefer not to consider some moods "good" and some "bad." We prefer "low" and "high" moods — although there is some danger in this terminology as well, especially with middle school students. In one sense, all moods could be considered "good" in that they serve a good purpose. For one thing, moods remind us of our humanness, and that is humbling. For another thing, the feelings we get from moods are like having an internal compass; that is, they are a way to tell if we are going in a productive direction for ourselves (gratitude, compassion, understanding), or an unproductive direction (anger, upset, frustration, disappointment) where we are an accident waiting to happen.

The truth is — and this is the key point about moods — moods are simply fluctuations in the quality of our thinking. Our thinking and our moods are so inextricably linked that there is no separating them. For our purposes, we don't need to know where moods come from. We accept them as a given. All we have to do is see ourselves in our moods, and act accordingly.

The most important thing that we can understand about moods is not to trust our thoughts when we are in low moods, because low moods are directly tied to low-quality thoughts. In a low mood our thoughts will tell us that our particular classroom of students is the worst in the history of education, that we were singled out among all teachers to get the worst class and it will always be this bad because we've got the worst luck of any ten people we know. In a high mood we're got a bunch of great kids and love our work. Same classroom, same kids. The only difference is a different mood talking. We have to learn not to take our low mood thinking so seriously.

An uncomfortable mood is like the red light on a car dashboard warning us that we're about to run out of oil and to stop and refill the oil before proceeding with caution. If we were sailing into a storm, we would do well to lower our sail and ride it out. Once the danger is passed, we can hoist the sail back up and proceed as normal. Low moods are warnings to back away from an impending fight, to doubt our thinking at those times, to resist the temptation to take a comment personally. If we understand this principle of how moods affect our ideas of life in the moment, then we will get through life more gracefully with less difficulty along the way and allow our well-being to return.

Low moods can be viewed as the wake-up call to clear our heads. It's a wonderful system, if we heed the warning.

B. Key Points

♦ Low moods mean that we are having low quality thoughts, that those thoughts can trick us, and we can't trust them.

♦ All we need to do in a low mood is to be patient, let it pass naturally, and wait it out before trying to make any major decisions or deal with problems.

♦ It is important to pay attention to what our moods are telling us, instead of paying attention to the seriousness of the thoughts we are getting in our low moods.

Sample Questions for Reflective Discussion

What is the relationship between your moods and the quality of your thinking?

Describe the kind of thinking you have in a low mood, and in a good mood. Does the same situation look the same? What do your moods tell you about whether you can trust your thinking at that time?

C. Needed Materials

a copy of the Mood Scale for each student [see end of session].

D. Opening Statement

ASK: From your home practice, where did your forks in the road take you?

[discussion]

In this session we're going to deal with something that everybody knows they have but most people do not understand: Moods!

E. Activity/Story Line

Before we talk about moods, we're going to do a little task.

[photocopy the next page as a worksheet and hand out to students; ask them to complete step one]

We're going to put this aside right now and pick it up later.

ASK: What are moods?

[entertain and acknowledge their ideas]

Do moods seem pretty mysterious to you? That's because they are. It's not really important to know what moods are. What is important is to know what to do when we have them.

ASK: Raise your hand if you have ever been in a bad mood or a low mood.

[If anybody's hand does not go up, ask if their friends would agree with them?]

So we all have moods. They rise and fall in us like the ocean has tides. A low mood comes upon us like a cloud passing across the sun.

ASK: When all we see up there are gray clouds, what happened to the sun?

[briefly entertain ideas]

It's always still there (just like our inner health). It just gets covered up by clouds, just as our inner wonderfulness gets covered by our low mood. If moods could be graphed they would look something like this:

TASK: Look at the mood scale. Look down the column to the left. Next to it, in column 1, place a check next to the item that best reflects your mood right now. Next, at the bottom of the page, after the number "1" write down whatever thoughts you are having now. Be honest with yourself.

MOOD SCALE

	1	2	3	4
I feel awesome				
Life is awesome!	____	____	____	____
Life is truly fascinating	____	____	____	____
I feel great	____	____	____	____
I feel pretty good	____	____	____	____
I feel okay	____	____	____	____
I'm neutral	____	____	____	____
I don't feel so good	____	____	____	____
I feel low	____	____	____	____
I feel really lousy	____	____	____	____
Don't bother me	____	____	____	____
I want out of life!	____	____	____	____

1. _____

2. _____

3. _____

4. _____

**[draw a straight line on the board, and over it draw squiggly lines
(something like a stock market performance chart)]**

neutral

We all go up and down in our moods all day long.

ASK: Have you noticed that some people are moodier than others? What do you think contributes to a person's moods?

Sometimes if we don't get much sleep, we feel low or crabby. Sometimes when we don't eat well we feel low. Sometimes if bad stuff happens we feel bad. But if we look closely we'll see that sometimes even when we haven't gotten much sleep or eaten well we'll feel okay, and sometimes when we *have* gotten enough sleep or are full we'll feel lousy. And we already learned that it's not stuff *out there* that causes us to feel certain ways, it's our thoughts — so it really comes back to our thoughts.

ASK: What are some of the things you've seen people do when people are in low moods that make the moods worse?

[entertain ideas]

Anyone who is human thinks more negatively in a low mood, even Cindy Crawford and Leonardo DiCaprio [substitute the names of the heartthrob of the day] and the President of the United States. What makes moods worse is acting on our thinking when we're in a low mood.

ASK: What does life look like to you when you are in a low mood?

[entertain ideas]

In a low mood we think low thoughts. Everything looks bad. School looks terrible. Our teachers are out to get us. Our friends look like they don't care about us or that they do stuff to us.

ASK: What does life look like to you when you are in a good mood, a high mood?

[entertain ideas]

In high moods we would say that our friend is nice. In low moods we might say that our friend is mean. Maybe it's because at those times our friend is in different moods — or maybe it's the mood we're in when we're seeing her or him.

ASK: What are some of the different thoughts you've had about your best friend?

[entertain ideas]

That's curious, isn't it? Why would we have those different kinds of thoughts? That's moods! In high moods we're so lucky to have friends like this; in low moods it's like, "With friends like this who needs enemies?"

ASK: What are some of the different thoughts you've had about school?

[entertain ideas]

In high moods, school isn't so bad, our teachers are okay. In low moods we curse the day we ever have to set foot in this school, our teachers don't care. They're nasty. The only difference is our low mood thinking.

That's interesting, isn't it? It's the same school, same teachers, same life.

[Note: Some students may say that school or a teacher always looks bad to them. That may be true, but if they looked closely they would see that even within what they call "bad," there is a range where on some days the teacher or school looks slightly better or worse than on other days. You might point this out.]

ASK: Raise your hands if you have a baby brother or sister. How many of you have seen them cry when they're in a low mood, and as soon as they get distracted they're laughing again?

Babies don't hold onto negative thoughts when they're in low moods. They drop them just like that, and then they're out of it into a different mood. They just let those thoughts go. Adults have forgotten how to do that. You students are probably in the process of forgetting that you can just let moods go and are starting to become like adults in this way — what a horrible thought! — except you'll be way ahead of most adults if you understand what moods are all about, which is what we're talking about now.

The good news is that low moods are temporary. They only last as long as we think about something bothersome. As soon as we get distracted and start thinking something else, our well-being automatically returns. All problems have solutions but we can only find them when our mind is cleared, and it is not clear in a low mood.

ASK: So what do you think this implies that we do when we're in a low mood?

[entertain ideas]

Nothing! In a low mood we should do nothing, or as little as we can get away with doing.

ASK: Knowing this, what do we want to do about the thinking we get in low moods?

[brief discussion]

Don't take this low mood thinking seriously. Especially, don't act on the thoughts we get in our low moods. And don't take personally what other people say to us when they're in low moods.

But we've also got to be careful about what we think when we're in what some of us call high moods. If we are really excited about something such as riding a roller coaster or taking drugs, and we wouldn't feel good without those things, we need to be a little suspicious of what we're calling a high mood. In this class, we are referring to a high mood as a natural, relaxed, peaceful, nice feeling state of mind.

On the other hand, we might be fooled into thinking that low moods are worthless. Not so! They are actually quite helpful to us. The feelings we get in low moods are those helpful signals we talked about. Have you ever noticed the lights that sometimes flash on a car's dashboard? They go on as a signal to the driver that something is wrong. It tells the driver to proceed with caution, or to stop altogether, depending on the light. The feelings we get from moods help us in the same way. They are our own internal signals to let us know when we should stop or proceed with caution.

In very low moods if we don't stop or proceed with caution we can get ourselves into a lot of trouble. These are the times when we are an accident waiting to happen. These are the times if we don't heed the internal warning signal, we'll start a fight, provoke someone else into anger, behave in a way that gets us into a problem, hurt someone's feelings, or hurt ourselves by doing something that's not in our best interest.

In a low mood Slick — remember him? — talks with a louder voice.

The problem is that what happens in a very low mood like that is we feel compelled to act. We are just dying to tell somebody off, or we are looking for a fight, or we are craving this thing we want, or we are driven to gorge ourselves with food, or we've got to take care of this right now no matter what, or we are so depressed that we even think about taking our life — BUT IT IS ONLY OUR MOOD TALKING, MAKING US FEEL COMPELLED. If people don't know this, and they believe what they think in a low mood, and if they follow the thinking that's compelling them, you can see where it could lead them into some serious difficulties. And people do these things often because they don't understand the meaning of moods for their lives.

ASK: What can we do once we've noticed the warning sign of low moods?

[brief discussion]

Know that our thinking is off and not act on it. We can't trust our low mood thinking. We're getting faulty messages at those times. The best thing we can do at that point is back off and relax or maybe do something nice for ourselves until our head clears and our mood rises. Then a problem we have will look completely different!

ASK: Let's go back to the mood scale. Place a check in column 2 next to the one item that best reflects your mood right now. Below, after #2, write down the thoughts you are having.

TASK: [Divide the class into groups of three] In your groups of three, talk about what your moods were, whether they changed and, if so, what the differences were. How was your thinking different?

F. Home Practice

At home when you get into a low mood, pull out the mood scale and do it again, using column 3 and the line numbered 3 below, filling in what thoughts you have. Then go do something nice for yourself, and after about twenty minutes or a half hour come back and fill it out one more time (column 4), and fill in line #4 below. See what, if any, insights you gained.

G. Summary

Ideally we want students to have the insight that if they get into a low mood, they can recognize it in themselves, and it tells them not to trust their thinking at those times. This is because in low moods they (and we) are always grinding away with computer-type thinking, recycling old, conditioned thoughts. In higher moods their (and our) thinking is fresh and new and uncontaminated. Knowing this, before they act, they can wait it out until their mood rises.

If we learn to see others in their moods, we can back off and not take personally what that person is doing, and wait for that person's mood to rise before dealing with them too much.

Session Eleven

Programmed Thinking

A. To Teachers

In this session we pick up on the notion of different world views, and take it further.

Sometimes we pick up ways of thinking, or patterns of thoughts and beliefs about ourselves and the world that, often without our knowing it, colors the way we see things. And for everyone it is different.

This has profound implications. Everyone is looking at the world through their own, very individualized, programmed thinking. Each of these thinking patterns tells that person what is important in life. Yet, it is different for everyone. Everyone thinks that different things in life are important.

One could say that each person's unique way of seeing the world is a little reality unto itself; that everyone lives in a "separate reality." No one else shares your reality because everyone's way of thinking is different. Everyone thinks that the things they think are really important because, of course everyone would see it that way. But everyone else does not see it that way — because they think other issues are important. Because of their different, separate ways of thinking.

It is as if we are each seeing the world with different colored glasses, forgetting we are wearing them, then trying to convince everyone else that our color is right. It is no wonder that people have such difficulty communicating.

As we'll see in this session, no one's way of seeing things is the "right" way. Everyone's way is a little skewed to show a particular point of view.

Consider the power of this realization. It has implications for all disagreements with others. It has implications for how we see people from diverse cultures and with diverse views. It has implications for how we respond when someone gets angry with us. It has implications for how we react when someone says we're not doing something right. Perhaps we do not have to take what other people are laying on us so personally; for it is only their own created "reality" talking.

At the same time it is also a message to take our own way of seeing things with a grain of salt. Perhaps we would be advised not to take our own selves so seriously, for it is only one way to see the world.

When our own programmed way of thinking is active and running it does not allow us to experience either the joy of the moment or learning in the moment. At those times our thoughts are rigidly focused on what we usually see. It cuts us off from taking in what life has to offer us anew in the moment because we are focused on what we think is the "right" way.

B. Key Points

◆ We each go through life as if different issues are important (for example, money, not getting pushed around, family, saving time, hard work, and so on) and whatever those issues are become our viewpoint, often without our realizing it, when we encounter nearly any situation.

◆ Our thinking patterns are self-confirming and self-validating; that is, without realizing it we go out of our way to fit even conflicting information into our own programming, so the way we see it always looks "right" to us.

◆ The more we are aware that we act out of our personalized ways of seeing things, and that others act out of theirs, the less we take personally what others say and do because it is only the way they happen to be seeing it (nor do we want to take our own unique thought-messages too seriously).

Sample Questions for Reflective Discussion

If you can program a computer, do you think you can program your mind?

Do you think your mind can ever get programmed without realizing it?

Can you tell what programs, or what habits of thinking, your computer runs for you? What about for your friends?

What do you think happens to your programmed thinking when you see your programmed thinking in action, that is, when you observe that thinking?

C. Needed Materials

Overhead or drawing of "Separate Realities" diagram (see end of session)

File cards, or cut up squares of paper (of approximately equal size and color)

D. Opening Statement

ASK: What did you discover about your moods and others' moods from your home practice?

[discussion]

In this session, we're going to be talking about another important piece of the picture, namely, the way we each see things differently.

We've talked a little about the fact that we each have different world views. This means that we all have different patterns of thoughts and beliefs about ourselves and the world that, often without our knowing it, color the way we see things. And for everyone it's different.

Don't expect to understand what this means yet. By the end of the session it should be clear.

E. Activity/Story Line

Consider this: every minute of every day, we have experiences created by our ability to think anything, and these experiences all get stored in our memories.

ASK: I'd like you all to close your eyes and put your head on your desk. With your eyes closed — without peeking — tell me what you remember seeing in this room. What color are the walls? What am I wearing and what color are my clothes? No peeking now!

[ask about other things.]

Okay, open your eyes. Since you couldn't see it, how would you know it if it wasn't in your memory?

This is what happens all day long. Every day, we take thousands and thousands of pieces of information through our senses and thinking into our brain, and it all gets stored in our memory.

ASK: How many different pieces of information (such as ideas, beliefs, names, numbers, impressions, pictures) do you think we have stored in our memory?

[briefly entertain suggestions without comment]

It's probably too high to count. But let's say we have trillions of pieces of information stored as thoughts in our brain.

ASK: Here's another question: How many things are on your mind at any one moment?

[again, briefly entertain suggestions]

Maybe one or a few at any one time.

ASK: Now, here's what's interesting: If we've got trillions of pieces of information stored in our memory, and we've only got one or a few thoughts on our mind at any given time, what do you think would be the odds of our having the same thought twice? Trillions here [point to the back of your head] and only a few here [point to front of your head].

The odds of having the same thought twice would be huge, almost impossible, wouldn't it? It would be far more unlikely than winning the lottery, more unlikely than having everyone you know win the lottery at the same time. Yet, we seem to have the same kinds of thoughts over and over again. And everyone else seems to have their same kinds of thoughts over and over again.

Isn't that interesting?

"We have our own habits of thinking that we have accumulated over the years that makes it look as if certain things are more important to us than other things. And those things are what we mostly end up thinking about."

What kind of thoughts does Slick, our mind traffic cop, pick out?

Slick, the traffic cop — our own typical way of thinking — picks out whatever it sees as relevant or important to us. We've picked up stuff over the years that we think is important. Those are the "important" thoughts that get put up on our mind-screen.

If we're alone in our house at night and we hear a banging sound, we might get scared. We keep hearing it and it seems to take over our mind. If we get up and look and see that it is just a branch from a tree that's banging on the house in the wind, we will go back and almost not hear it any more, because it is no longer relevant or important to us. If someone else comes in, they'll say, "What's that noise?" And you'll say, "Oh, that's just a branch, " and the other person will say, "Oh, okay."

When something is no longer relevant or important to us, we barely hear it any more.

ASK: Where do you think your distinct way of thinking comes from? Where do you get your ideas about what is important?

[discussion]

Mostly, we get our ideas of what is important from our parents' ideas about what is important. We have picked those things up from our parents, often without knowing about them. So our way of thinking gets what it knows from the messages it receives from our parents — a lot by how we are treated as we grow up. We take these messages in through our thoughts and they shape us into who we are today. Our close relatives and our teachers and our peers also give us messages, and we have all kinds of experiences. It all gets incorporated into our own way of thinking in the same way that a computer gets programmed, and it helps us to make sense out of the world.

So, mostly, we are taught our programming from our parents, and our parents were taught their programming from their parents, and their parents were taught their programming by their parents, and so forth. Every time it is passed along it changes somewhat, but we would all be surprised to see how much of our programming we got from our parents.

So our parents taught our Slick traffic cop what life is all about, about what the important issues are in life, made it part of our own way of thinking.

Some of our parents taught us life is all about money. So they see everything in terms of whether they can afford it, or whether something is too expensive. When someone says, let's go somewhere, they'll say, "How much will it cost?" Everything gets seen in terms of money. Others were taught, life is all about "not backing down from anyone." Others were taught, life is all about "hard work." Others were taught, life is all about "what you can get away with." Others were taught, life is about "being afraid." Or "life is about seeing what's beautiful, or new." Or life is about "helping people who are less fortunate," or whatever.

TASK: What did your parents teach you about what life is all about, what the important issues are in life? No, don't tell me now. Pair up with a person sitting next to you, and talk about what you got from your parents about what life is all about.

[give them about 5 minutes]

TASK: Now, as an experiment, without writing down your names, everyone write down one word or one phrase that describes what you got from your parents about what life is all about. So I want you to fill in this blank:

[write on the board:]

"Life is all about_____." [for example, some would say, "making money," some would say, "hard work," some would say, "being mean."]

[The students fill in the blank. This should take no more than thirty seconds.]

[Collect the cards. After they're handed in, shuffle the cards or mix up the papers, then read through them quickly: Say, "Life is all about_____." and say their words or phrases.]

Isn't this fascinating?! The important things in life are different for most everyone. And even where they are the same, if we got into the details we would probably find that it was a little different.

There are at least four fascinating things about this:

ASK: Because what is important about life is different for everyone, which answer is "right?"

[discussion]

None of them! Or all of them equally. Everything that comes from our separate ways of thinking is no better or no worse than what comes from anyone else's — unless it involves hurting other people or things. Everyone is simply looking at the world through different colored glasses.

True story: One day two couples went out camping in the woods. One guy was usually very easy going, but when he got to the campsite he suddenly wanted everyone to get going and get wood so they could start the fire. Everyone else was puzzled by the guy's anxiety, but the other fellow went along with him to get wood. He wanted to stop and see the beautiful scenery but the first guy wouldn't let him. "No, we've got to get going, get this wood, and get back and make a fire." So they got back to the campsite and the guy tried to hurry his wife along to get moving, but she was lying down reading. She said, "No, I'm really not ready to move right now." Then she looked up at him and asked, "Hey, why do you have your sunglasses on?" And he put his hand up to his eyes and said, "Oh!" He took his sunglasses off, which he didn't know he had on, and said, "Oh, it's early!"

The guy saw everything through his shades without knowing he had them on. He thought that it was getting dark, which meant that it was getting late, and it made him want to hurry everyone up. All this because he didn't know he had sunglasses on.

But here's the kicker: this is the way all of us humans are all the time. We all go through life as if we have different colored shades on. Without knowing we have them on, we see everything through them, and then we feel certain ways because of them. And we act as if that's what everyone else sees.

Those different colored shades are our own ways of thinking.

ASK: Have you ever put on an funny-colored pair of sunglasses? What happens when you have them on for a while?

[briefly entertain ideas]

At first when you put them on everything looks really weird, but if you leave them on for an hour or so, everything begins to look normal. We only realize it's not normal when we take them off.

That's what our programmed thinking does to us. So everyone is walking around thinking that their way is normal and right and, of course everyone else would see it the same way. But everyone is seeing it in a different way, each person thinking that his or her way is normal and right.

That's why there are so many fights, arguments, and disagreements in the world. In fact, it's the only reason people argue and fight. They don't realize that everyone is walking around in a separate world where they all see things differently.

Here's the second interesting point: For every thought about what's important that we know about (like the ones you wrote on your papers) there's at least another one that we don't know about. But our friends could tell us. This is what we call a "blindspot." We're so close to it that we can't even see it, but it's still part of what Slick is letting onto our screen.

For example, our blindspot might be:"Life is all about trying to feel okay about myself in comparison to others." So every time that person is in a situation where he feels uncomfortable, he may put someone down or make fun of them so he'll look more cool. He doesn't realize he is doing it. The whole rest of the class knows that's what he does, but the person himself can't see it. And everyone has their own stuff that they don't see.

Here's a third interesting point: Every time we hear something, we try to fit it into what our programming is.

For example, if our habits of thinking tell us:"Life is all about not being fat," that person will look at everything through the eyes of whether it makes them look skinny or not. Let's say a girl thinks she's fat. She goes to her friend and asks, "Do you think I'm fat?" If her friend says, "Yeah, you could probably lose a little weight," she would probably say, "I knew it!" If her friend says,"No, I don't think you're fat," the girl won't believe it, or she will think her friend is lying to her, or that she is just trying to be nice to her. Either way, she still comes out thinking she's fat because that's what her belief system tells her. So it doesn't matter what the answer is, Slick somehow tries to make it fit into what she already believes.

Perhaps the best way to see this is with anorexia. Someone with anorexia can stand in front of a mirror, bone skinny, and see herself as fat. Anyone else who sees her would think she was nuts; she is totally skinny! And they would try to tell the anorexic girl that she was skinny, not fat, so skinny in fact that she sometimes looks like a skeleton with skin on it. But the anorexic person doesn't believe it because she sees herself as fat, and no one can talk her out of it.

Someone with bulimia may not see herself to be quite as fat as an anorexic, or maybe she just wants to make sure she doesn't get fat. But she also wants to eat. So, given the way she sees it, she gorges herself, then may stick her finger down her throat to throw up.

It's like if you were at a fun house in the circus and looked in one of the distorted mirrors, and you saw yourself as really fat, and then believed it and started starving yourself or gorging and purging because of it.

But this is the way we all are with our own computer-programmed thinking. We all act based on the way we see it. It is only a matter of extremes.

Our way of thinking creates our own outlook, and then we act based on how things look to us.

ASK: Can anyone see how this might limit us?

[briefly entertain ideas without comment]

Let's say you were with a group of your friends, and that group always talked about how they didn't like a particular kid. They don't want that kid hanging out with them. Suppose later you bumped into that kid and she started talking to you and you started to think, "Gee, she isn't so bad after all. She's pretty nice. Why haven't we been hanging out with her?" This is an example of how a mind-set can limit you. The group was seeing through a distorted lens about this kid, then they acted on the distortion.

ASK: Suppose someone carried with them the mindset, "I can't back down from anyone." What do you think that person might get involved in?

[briefly entertain ideas]

A lot of fights.

ASK: Suppose someone carried with them the mindset, "It's important that people pay attention to me." What do you think that person might do?

[briefly entertain ideas]

See, the problem is, they can't see what they're doing, and you can't see what you're doing, and I can't see what I'm doing. We are all alike in this respect — it just comes out differently, and in some a lot worse than others. Some people's thinking even leads them into severe dangers when they're not aware of the role their thoughts play in their lives.

ASK: What do you think this means for your own life?

[discussion]

Unless we see it, there's nothing much we can do about it. So the first thing is, we want to recognize that we all have programmed ways of thinking that we operate from.

If we're in an argument with someone, we can recognize that's just the way they see it, and our view is just the way we see it. They think what we're saying and doing is crazy, and we think what they're saying and doing is crazy.

Maybe that means we don't have to take what others throw at us too personally. If someone tells us that we're no good, it's just their thoughts talking, and they probably don't even know what they're doing — so why would we want to take that personally? And even if they did know what they were doing, that's the way they see it. It's a distortion. Like a distorted pair of glasses, it makes us see things differently, and then we feel and do things differently when we don't know any better at the time.

And we are the same way as the person who puts us down. We just do it about different things and in different ways. Slick is still calling the shots. They are just different shots.

ASK:: Does anyone have any ideas about what we can do to take the power out of our own oersonal thinking that has such a hold on us?"

[discussion]

[show picture of separate realities]

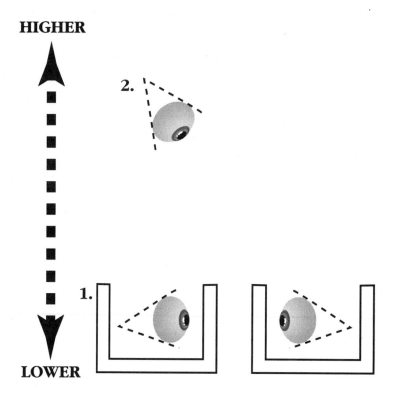

Just watch ourselves and others doing it! Observe! See people in the act of thinking their personal, unique thoughts, and watch how these questionable thoughts lead to an action. Also, watch your own programmed thinking tell you how to see thing and take things. And none of your ideas, or our ideas, are any better than anyone else's so long as it does no harm.

When we step back and observe, we give Cool a moment to zip in with some perspective and wisdom.

And this leads us to the fourth and perhaps most important point:

There is nothing cast in stone about the way we have been programmed to think. Slick is only a set of thoughts, and thoughts can change like the wind. Each thought is a new way of being — if we are aware of it. We are never locked into the way we think we are, any more than a computer is locked into one program. We can always change our minds.

[Write on the board]

TRUST YOUR WISDOM and distrust the same old thoughts we get all the time.

And remember, Cool wisdom only comes with a clear head.

F. Home Practice

Become detectives. Watch other people and see if you see what their Slick-type thinking is telling them, and see if they act out what Slick, the traffic cop, tells them.

G. Summary

Ideally, after this session the students would say to themselves: "Whoa, you mean I took on this way of seeing things from my folks or someone, and everyone sees those things differently? And that's what I've been carrying around in my head that I think is so important, and that is what I act out of?! That means I can't really take myself too seriously or take what other people tell me personally, because of course they're going to say what they say and do what they do given how they see things." But it can all change with new, fresh thinking.

HIGHER

2.

1.

LOWER

Session Twelve

Levels of Understanding

A. To Teachers

In the past two sessions we have seen that 1) the same situation can look completely different depending on our mood, and 2) whatever we see is colored by our perspective or world view. We will now take it a step further: 3) every situation we encounter can be seen from a great variety of different perspectives. Although not often obvious to us at the time, it is possible to see any situation from a higher level of perspective, or with more detachment.

People can have vertical leaps of understanding that help them see with far greater clarity than they do now.

B. Key Points

◆ At any given moment, we are a certain distance away from our health or from healthy functioning.

◆ Any fixed event can be seen from a variety of levels of understanding.

◆ Once people understand that in any situation there are many possibilities other than the way they are seeing it at the moment, they become open to seeing new possibilities.

Sample Questions for Reflective Discussion

Have you ever noticed that your perspective about something changed, or that someone else's had? Describe it. What do you think made that change in perspective happen?

What does it feel like to see something in a way you never thought of before?

Why is it that in the same situation, such as seeing a kid get picked on by a bully, one person will feel anger, another will get worried, another will find it funny, another will feel compassion, etc? What do you make of that?

What makes people see the same situation differently? Which one is right? Which one is "the way it really is?"

Can the way you see a situation ever change? How?

If you were lost in the woods and someone lifted you up in a helicopter, do you think you'd see your situation differently? If you were lost in a problem and were lifted up so you could look down at it instead of being stuck in the middle of it, do you think you'd see the problem differently?

C. Needed Materials

Two overheads [or write them on newsprint or on the board (as they appear at the end of this session) but have them covered up]: "When we don't like what someone else is doing" and "Remembering a painful event." These could also be given out as handouts after the class.

D. Opening Statement

In your home practice you looked at how different people see things differently.

ASK: What did you discover about this?

[discussion]

Today we're going to talk about a new way of seeing things.

You're lost in the woods. You can't see your way out. You don't have the slightest idea where you are or how to get to your destination. All you can see is trees. You have no idea where to turn. You start to get worried. You start running but trip over a branch and land flat on your face. You start to panic.

You then look up and see a very tall tree. You begin to climb it. You climb up and up until you can see the tops of the trees. Things look different from up there. You can't quite see beyond the woods but you see a dip, a crevice in the tree line. It could be a stream! Maybe you should go in that direction and follow it.

But wait, you spot a helicopter flying by. You wave at it and shout. It sees you. It hovers overhead and drops a line down toward you. You grab it and it lifts you up. Up above the trees you go. You can now see that what you were looking at was, in fact, a stream. The helicopter lifts you higher. You can now see a road. It lifts you higher still. You can now see the edge of the forest. It lifts you higher still. You can see where you wanted to go! Had you been able to see from that level in the first place, you would have known exactly where to go. You wouldn't have panicked. You feel great!

No matter what situation we find ourselves in, we can have a similar experience to either being lost in the woods or having a helicopter come along. This can happen in any event we encounter. We now see the situation in a certain way. We think that is the only way to see it, the only way to experience it. Yet, if we only had a higher perspective, like being able to see the woods from above, we would see it differently than we do now and, therefore, have a different experience.

We can always see anything from a different perspective than we do now.

E. Activity/Story Line

True story: During the 1995 NBA Basketball Playoffs, the San Antonio Spurs were favored to beat the Houston Rockets. They had the best record in the league, largely due to their captain, 7'1" center, David Robinson, and to the league's best rebounder and defender, Dennis Rodman. The problem was, Dennis Rodman was kind of a loose cannon. Not only does he dye his hair many colors, not only does he have tattoos all over his body, not only did he date Madonna, but in a game during a "time out" he would sometimes sit apart from his team at the end of the bench and not listen to the coach. Sometimes he would even take his sneakers off indicating that he was disgusted and was not going back into the game.

In the playoffs, during a crucial game, with only a few seconds left on the clock and the score tied, Houston got the ball and called time out. Dennis Rodman sat down at the end of the bench apart from his team, not listening to his coach. The team went back on the court for the last play of the game. Dennis Rodman missed his defensive assignment. The man he was supposed to be guarding scored, and San Antonio lost the game (and later the series).

Newspaper reporters, other coaches, and fans were all up in arms, shouting, "Rodman should be benched!" "Rodman should be traded!" "He's no good for the team!"

In an interview the next day team captain David Robinson was asked whether he thought Rodman should be benched or traded.

Robinson said, "See, people don't understand, Dennis Rodman is part of our team. We've got to understand him. We've got to find a way to bring him in. We've got to love him. That's what being a team of people is all about."

Everyone in the audience was shocked by his response.

ASK: What made David Robinson see Dennis Rodman so differently from everyone else?

[brief discussion]

No one knows why, because no one is inside David Robinson's head. All we can say is that he was seeing the situation from a higher level of understanding, or from a deeper perspective, than anyone else.

It was like David Robinson was up in a helicopter looking at the bigger picture, and everyone else was in the woods, caught up in their own little reactions to Dennis Rodman.

True story: One of the authors of this curriculum was asked to give a speech to an agency in upstate New York. He arrived the night before and stayed over in a motel. When he got up in the morning he looked at his information to tell him where he was supposed to go to give the speech, and nothing in the material he had told him where he was supposed to go. He had no idea where his session was supposed to be held.

Fear set in. He started to panic. "Oh no! What am I going to do? I'm going to let these people down!"

Almost instantly it was followed by a feeling of anger, "How could those people have let me leave my office without telling me where I was supposed to go?"

Again, almost instantly this thought was followed by, "What a fool! How could I have left my office without knowing where I was supposed to go?"

Suddenly he realized that he had just experienced the same situation from three completely different feelings: fear, anger, and feeling like a fool. That meant he was seeing the same situation in three different ways, from three different perspectives. Each way he saw it produced a different feeling in him, and had he acted on any of them he would have acted differently, depending on which level he was at.

Then he realized, "Hey! If I could see this situation at three different levels, and they're all low levels, I wonder if I could see this situation from higher levels, from different perspectives?"

Then he thought, "Well, this agency hired me because they were having problems, so maybe they couldn't even get it together to get me what I needed." Lo and behold, his feeling began to change. He felt compassion. He felt his mood begin to rise.

Next, the thought popped into his head, "Hey, I could see this as a challenge. I could be like a detective to find out where I'm supposed to go." He felt his mood level rise higher.

He made his way to a nearby college campus. He only remembered that the job had something to do with a college. He began asking people from various offices on the campus to find anyone who might know where his session was. Nobody did at first, but they sent him to someone else who might know, and he began to get some clues. As he was walking across the campus, it was such a gorgeous, crisp, clear, sunny day, that the thought popped up to him, "Boy, if I had known where I was supposed to go, and simply drove there and walked in the door, I wouldn't be out here experiencing this beautiful day like this, and not only that, but I wouldn't have realized what I realized about levels of understanding." By the time he found where he was supposed to be, he was feeling great. His talk went beautifully.

ASK: What do you think is important about this?

[discussion]

The message is, nothing about the situation changed. It was exactly the same. The only thing different was how he was seeing it. At first he saw it at very low levels and had low feelings associated with it. When his perspective rose higher, his feelings improved.

It is possible to see any situation from many different levels of perspective.

But something else is important about this: What the man didn't realize at the time was that he didn't need to go out of his way to try to change the way that he saw the situation in order to raise his level of understanding. All he needed to realize was that there were other possibilities of how he could see it other than the way he was seeing it — there are always other possible ways to see it! — and that some ways produce healthier feelings than other ways. All he had to do was to realize that what he thought was "real" — that he was seeing it the way it really was — wasn't "real" at all. He only thought it was "real" because he was seeing it that way. Simply knowing that every situation presents an endless variety of possibilities from which it is possible to see frees us up from being locked in to the way we feel at that time.

Here is a story about someone from another school: all through elementary school Sara was part of a group of friends who hung around together. As they were growing up, though, Nicole, who was kind of the leader of the group, would give her a hard time every once in a while. Now that they entered a much larger middle school, Nicole became friends with another group. She then invited all the rest of the kids from her elementary school group to join them — except Sara. In fact, every time Nicole would see Sara when she was with her new group, Nicole would start picking on her and making fun of her. Under Nicole's influence the rest of Sara's friends began to drift away from Sara. Sara became very sad, then she began to feel insecure. She started to hate Nicole and what she was doing to her.

ASK: What do you think Sara's thoughts were about Nicole? How was Sara seeing Nicole?

[briefly entertain ideas without comment]

ASK: How do you think that made her feel?

[again, briefly entertain ideas]

ASK: Feeling that way, what do you think Sara would do?

[again]

ASK: Do you think there are any other possible ways that Sara could see Nicole? What are they?

[Write down their responses on the board — but when you write them down, without saying anything about them, if you think they are pretty high level responses write them high on the board (for example, seeing the other person with compassion, or seeing a larger context), if they're pretty low level responses (for example, taking it personally or getting upset) write them low on the board, and if they're in between write them in the middle. The chart below will help you see some of the possible responses. This exercise may be difficult for the students, but that's okay. They might have a tendency to suggest what Sara might do, but that's not what you're asking. If they are stuck, try to refrain from giving them any hints or examples. Instead, say things like, "You mean this is the only possible way to see it?" or "Are there any other possible ways to see this?" After they've run out of responses, you can ask —]

ASK: [starting from the lowest response and then moving higher, point to the response and ask] If Sara saw it this way, how would she feel? For example, if Sara saw Nicole as "out to get her," how would she feel?

[briefly entertain ideas]

[*Then move up the ladder of responses and ask the same question of each (of each one that looks important to you)*.] For example, if Sara saw Nicole as "someone who was insecure herself and didn't know how to make friends without putting someone else down," how would Sara feel?

Here is a summary of only some of the possible ways that people can see this kind of situation:

[Reveal the chart, "When We Don't Like What Someone Is Doing." (You will find it at the end of this session.) Show one statement at a time, beginning with the bottom statement, by covering up all the other statements above it. Then, move the cover up one statement at a time to reveal the next one above it.]

Some Possible Levels To See Someone When We Don't Like What S/he Is Doing

◆ see it with amusement

"It's so funny what some people will do to others in this world! It's like watching a 'sit-com'!"

◆ see their insecurity behind their behavior and feel compassion

◆ see that maybe you once did something that hurt others and feel humility

◆ find what they're doing interesting and accept it

◆ be bothered by their unacceptable behavior

◆ get upset at their intentions

◆ take it personally

These are all possibilities. Each one produces a different feeling.

There is no right or wrong way to see it. This simply means that since you're the ones that have to carry around these feelings, you actually have more power to decide which of these feelings you'll have, since you can ask yourself to want to see it at a higher level. Or you can wait until you're simply seeing it at a higher level later on, naturally.

It is even possible to see this in terms of hanging out at the mall. Why is it that some people seem to have a better time than others when hanging out at the mall? Or, sometimes we have a really good time there and at other times we don't. What's going on?

Could it be that there are different ways to see hanging out at the mall which, depending on how we see it, could determine how we feel about it?

ASK: When you go to the mall to hang out, what are some things that you want to have happen?

[This time don't write them, just entertain ideas.]

ASK: What do you think the difference would be if you went to the mall with these different expectations?

[write the following statements on the board, from the bottom up]

[write this statement low on the board:] I'm going to meet a cute guy there.

[write this one higher:] I'm going there to look at cute guys.

[write this one still higher:] I'm going to let whatever happens happen and just watch and appreciate it.

Is it possible that the expectation you have might have something to do with how you end up feeling about it?

*[simply let this question set for a moment to let it sink in.
If anyone has anything to say, fine, but otherwise move on.]*

It is even possible to see any event — any painful event that happened to you, from lots of different levels. [*Reveal the "Remembering a Painful Event" chart, one level at a time, again covering up all other statements except the bottom level, then move the cover up one at a time.*]

Some Possible Ways To See A Painful Event
That Comes Into Our Memory

◆ Something even better might come out of it.

◆ It's a turning point; before I didn't see other possibilities.

◆ I learned from it.

◆ Things happen, sometimes lousy things, but I'm not going to let it ruin my life.

◆ It left a scar. I'm "damaged goods."

◆ It ruined my life.

How you feel it is determined by how you see it. And each person gets what they see. Again, this does not mean that we "should" be seeing it from a higher level. It only means that whatever level we do see it at determines how we end up feeling about it. And there are always higher-level possibilities.

[pause, and let it sink in]

Given the level you are seeing something at, you are always doing the best you know how at the time.

This also means that everyone else is doing the best that they know how at the time, given the way they see it. This includes your parents and your teachers — everyone!

ASK: What meaning does this have for our lives?

[discussion. If they are having trouble coming up with something, ask —]

ASK: What does this mean about the needs, wants and desires we have?

[entertain ideas]

This means that our needs, wants, and desires that we experience at one level, which we consider very real, would not necessarily be considered needs, wants and desires if we saw them at another level. For example, if we need to have some cute guy to go out with right now, and then we get involved with our friends, we will forget about that "need" — until we start to think about it in that way again. These needs and desires are really like mirages. You know what a mirage is, right? Like if we're driving in the car on a blistering hot day and we think we see water on the road in front of us but when we get up to that place it's not really there. When we get up close to it, we discover that it is not "real," even though it sure looked real. So what we consider to be something we need is really only something that we think is a need at that time. But through our thinking we continually experience things differently, and then we experience the effects of whatever thinking we have and the something else feels "real." This is the game of life that we play, without being aware of it.

So when we're down in the dumps about something, or we really want something that we can't have and we feel bad about it, the more we can see it as something we've made up, and that we could just as possibly make up something else, the better it might make us feel. The better we feel, the closer we are to our health. At the very least, we'll feel less awful.

Remember, we don't need to go out of our way to make up anything else! All we really need to do is see it for what it is: that how we're seeing it now is just one of many possible levels of understanding, and there are very likely other higher perspectives that we could have. Simply knowing this can help us.

F. Home Practice

When you experience any low feelings in the next week that appear to be caused by a situation you're experiencing, or by some person, ask yourself how you're seeing the situation or person now, then ask yourself whether there might be other possible ways to see it from a higher level of understanding. Don't analyze it; just see what comes to you.

G. Summary

Life is really a series of levels of understanding. No single event or situation in life can only be seen in one way.

Ideally, we would hope that the students have an insight such as, "Wait a minute, there are lots of other ways to look at this situation (or person) other than the way I'm seeing it now — a world of possibilities that I haven't yet even dreamed of — that could give me a better feeling. A better feeling usually means that I'm closer to my health. And, because other people are seeing their situations from whatever levels they're seeing things at, that means they're always doing the best they know how to do at the time, given how they're seeing it. Me too! But now that I know there are other levels, that means I'm no longer locked into the feelings I'm having about something."

Session Thirteen

Our Innate Health:
Healthy Mental Functioning And How To Access It

A. To Teachers

Throughout this curriculum, we've been pointing in the direction of healthy mental functioning which is the way we use our minds to experience well-being. One way to look at it is that healthy functioning is the proper use of our thinking so that we can access our wisdom and common sense.

Another way to see this is that our mental functioning is naturally healthy in the absence of low quality thinking when our heads are clear. In this session we will cover what healthy functioning is and how to access it; why clearing the head is so good for us; what results we can expect; what it feels like; and how to do it.

What does healthy psychological functioning look like? It is a life free of overwhelming stress. If we are regularly stressed out, we are not functioning in a mentally healthy way. If we generally feel a sense of well-being, we are in healthy functioning.

How does one gain healthy psychological functioning? The path is a clear head and the right use of our minds at the right time. In a sense, this session puts together everything we have discussed thus far.

Why does having a clear head give us healthy, wise, commonsense, productive thoughts? Once again, this is one of the mysteries of the universe, but it certainly looks as if our health is natural to us, that it's innate. We only think ourselves away from it. That's why, when our heads clear, we get healthy thoughts. The healthy thinking pops to the surface like a cork that had been held under water.

When you, the teacher, see the value of healthy functioning and the merits of a clear head you will best be able to convey to students that it is something to cherish and nurture. This curriculum has pointed in this direction, so you may well already see it. For your review, we've provided a summary to aid in further reflection.

Society does not necessarily support the concepts and processes used in this curriculum. In other words, society often pushes for heavy, analytic thinking, suggesting that figuring out one's problems and mulling things over is beneficial. Actually, the only time this process works well is when we are engaged in a task such as figuring out what groceries to buy for the cake we want to bake, balancing our checkbooks, figuring out a budget, etc. The ability to calculate and analyze is very helpful in these areas. It is not helpful to analyze when we want a free flow of fresh thought to inspire our students to learn the day's lesson plan. If we have a lot weighing on our minds we won't be inspired — unless we can forget about it, at least for the class period.

When we know what all the variables are, then it is helpful to us to process and analyze. When we don't know all the variables, we need fresh solutions. When all the variables that will help us solve a problem are not known, processing and analyzing only make us spin our wheels.

You can probably recall a time or two when you weren't thinking about anything in particular and an important idea came to mind. Perhaps it was an obvious solution to a problem you had put in the back of your mind — some people call it the "back burner" — or maybe what popped to mind helped make your day go a little smoother, or perhaps it was a creative, new lesson plan. That is what happens when your head is clear of heavy, burdensome thoughts.

People do some of their best thinking when they are not purposely thinking. This is the power of our intrinsic wisdom. Our intelligence goes much deeper than the list of facts we memorized a day or so ago. When our heads are clear we have a direct, open path for that deeper intelligence to come through. When our minds are clear we can see the "big picture," we don't have to take things personally, we don't react to what someone else has said (or if we do, we recognize that our thinking is "off" at that moment), we have access to common sense and a deeper understanding, and we see people's behaviors more as the result of their "thought-induced state," rather than taking it personally.

The more we get used to clearing our heads, and trusting that starting point, the more we accomplish. When our minds are busy with a lot of mental chatter we miss opportunities that we otherwise may have discovered.

When our minds are clear it feels as if there is more space between thoughts. We become more aware of our surroundings and are more available to others. When our minds are clear it is a lot easier to see where to go next. The obvious becomes apparent, where before it was covered, obscured, by a lot of extraneous thoughts. Our thoughts can bring harmony or disharmony into our lives, and we are responsible for what we think. Actually, that's not entirely correct, because we find that we can't seem to control a lot of what we think. A more correct statement is that we are responsible for what we do with our thinking. We are responsible for which thinking to trust and follow. We can be responsible for helping our minds become more calm so we get higher quality thoughts.

To clear our heads we do not have to go on vacation or jump in our cars or in the shower. There are easier ways. Sometimes simply having the desire to clear our heads is all it takes. Sometimes, just saying, "I don't know," will clear our heads. At other times, when we're really bogged down with heavy thoughts that we can't seem to turn off it becomes more challenging. Sometimes it helps to distract our minds by doing something physical that is relatively mindless, or find something to distract our heavy thoughts. But it's no guarantee. If we get the same kinds of distracting thoughts coming into our heads all the time we can say to ourselves something like, "These are not the kinds of things I want on my mind" — and we can discredit those thoughts whenever they arise.

What can help is to be absolutely committed to living our lives with less stress and increasingly from a clear mind. This will help meet the challenge of our busy, cluttered minds with renewed strength and hope. It can be a standard we set for ourselves. We want to move our standard up a notch, and not be satisfied to live okay-but-stressed-out lives.

Have you ever been in line at the grocery store immersed in heavy thoughts about the horrors of wasted time and how you wish that slow people would have their own designated check-out line, and your mind is burdened with these distressing thoughts, then all of a sudden you realize that you can read a magazine until it's your turn. Lo and behold when it is your turn, having completely forgotten about "slow people" you reluctantly set the magazine aside that you were so engrossed in. This is how much life itself seems to change when our heads clear from all the personal thoughts we get wrapped up in. And it is only different thinking.

Remember, nothing we can "do" is guaranteed to clear our heads. The idea is to do whatever we need to do to get our heads clear. If we have time we might try to do an activity we truly enjoy such as jog, walk, play music, fish, tinker under the hood of the car, garden, etc. If we do not have time, we could think of something funny, or close our eyes for a moment and breathe or do a brief meditation. Whatever we wind up doing, the point is to distract our minds long enough to slip into more receptive thinking and, hence, a quieter frame of mind. Once we are out of the muck and mire of fast, heavy thinking we can constantly make it our business to revisit there.

But it is not solely the activity that changes our thinking! It is looking in the wrong direction to think that if we could only do a certain activity our heads would clear. The possibility of a calm mind always exists for us at every moment. That possibility is inside us already. We're only using the activity or the practice as an excuse to bring out what already resides in us. For example, the idea is not to do meditation, the idea is to be in a meditative state, which the practice of meditation sometimes helps some people achieve — but sometimes it doesn't. Many times during the day we go in and out of a meditative state. It can be while doing the dishes. It can be anywhere, any time. It does not depend on any act or practice. It is within and always available.

It is a good thing we are wired up in a way that allows us to clear our heads, since that is the space we can really trust. No one hurts another when his or her head is clear; nor do we torture ourselves with unhappy, heavy thoughts when we're clear-headed. A calm mind, a clear head is the antidote to problems.

At this point you might be saying, "Well, don't you have to think problems out? Otherwise, how would you ever think of a solution?" On the surface this sounds right, but it is a myth. As Albert Einstein said, you can't solve a problem from the same level of thought that created it. We have to be outside the problem — not in it — to see a fresh perspective, where uncontaminated "solution thoughts" reside.

Everyone possesses this miraculous, perfect, wise place inside themselves. We periodically contact it by accident. It is possible to contact this inner treasure more often for longer periods — if we know where it resides.

You might want to practice clearing your head on your own for a while before teaching this lesson to students. Enjoy the peace and quiet that you'll find from a quiet, clear mind, and then you will want to give this gift to others, including your students.

It is possible for almost anyone to live in a state of healthy psychological functioning.

B. Key Points

◆ Healthy functioning is, essentially, living a life not burdened by a lot of stress. It is available to everyone naturally, in the absence of unhealthy thinking.

◆ A clear head is perhaps the most valuable gift we can give ourselves, since it is the opening to our deeper wisdom.

◆ We can recognize a clear head by the feeling of security, tranquillity and peace that accompanies it.

Sample Questions for Reflective Discussion

When do you think people are at their best?

When are you at your best?

If you let your healthy, clear-headed thinking rise up in you naturally without letting the other thinking hold it down, what do you think would happen in your life?

What do you think is the most valuable gift you can give yourself for your mental health?

What does a clear, calm mind do for your mental health?

What's the difference in how you feel, and what you do, when your mind is calm, compared with when it isn't? What implications does this have for your life?

C. Needed Materials

paper and pen or pencil

diagram 1: innate health (see end of session) [*Note: Ideally, it would be best to make overheads of these if you have access to an overhead projector, but it can be drawn on a board as well.*]

diagram 2: innate health and the thinking that obscures it (see end of session)

D. Opening Statement

ASK: What did you discover in your home practice about opening up to the possibility of a higher perspective?

[brief discussion]

This session will help us see what kind of life we want to lead, and how natural it is because it is already part of us. Do we want to live a life where we're stressed out a lot of the time, or would we rather that our lives feel peaceful and wise and happy? This is called a feeling of well-being. It happens when our mind functions in a healthy way. It happens when the health that resides in us pops up to the surface. This healthy functioning of the mind is available to each of us.

It's a treasure.

Did you ever imagine that you'd be learning how to clear your head in school? Isn't that the place we go to fill our heads?

School teaches us facts, figures, historical events, etc. It's important and quite helpful to know the difference between an inch and a yard if you're about to make a dress or put a stock car together. It is equally helpful to know the difference between a teaspoon and a tablespoon if you're about to make chocolate milk. You get the idea.

Problems arise when our head is filled with so much stuff that it is jumbled and we are getting affected by a lot of personal thoughts. You know, the kind of thinking that creates rumors, lies, anger, hostility, jealousy, resentment. We could call this heavy, burdened, taking-it-personally thinking. This is the domain of Mr. Slick, remember? That kind of thinking keeps us from experiencing our health.

E. Activity/Story Line

Here is a diagram that attempts to summarize everything we've been talking about so far. Of course, the diagram is only a representation of something that can't really be represented, so the idea is not the diagram itself (because it could be off a little), its importance is the meaning behind the diagram.

Let's say that here is our health.

[point to diagram 1: Innate Health]

It's innate — it's part of us. We're either born with it or we just have access to it at any moment. It doesn't matter which it is. But it's always available to us.

Our innate health contains natural self-esteem, natural mental health, natural peace of mind, natural deep feelings like love and joy, and a natural intelligence that contains wisdom and common sense.

Everyone has this within them.

ASK: If this is in everyone, why then do most people walk around looking like they don't have it and maybe never could?

[entertain ideas]

Because we start to think in ways that cover it up, that obscure it from our view.

[replace first diagram with diagram 2]

So we pick up ways of thinking as we grow that make us afraid, angry, jealous, worried, bothered by others, make us blame others or other things, give us beliefs about things, give us our ego that we feel like we need to protect — and lots more.

As long as all that kind of thinking is there, we can't see or be in touch with the health in us. So it looks like it's not there at those times. But it really is. It's just like the sun on a rainy day that we had talked about. It's still there even though we can't see it at the time.

So sometimes we're connected to our health **[point to health]**, and sometimes we're lost in our anger, fear, worry, bother, etc. **[point to bottom of the outside circle]** and lots of levels in between.

[point to line on the diagram 2 that looks like a thermometer or a ladder: Innate Health and The Thinking That Obscures It]

So these levels could represent the mood we're in at any given time, and they could represent what we talked about last session, that is, the possible levels of understanding in which we can see any situation, or it could also represent the level of life that we generally live in. In other words, some people generally live lives of fear, or lives of anger, or lives of depression (there are variations but they usually fall within a general range), and some people live generally happy, healthy lives, and lots of levels in between.

But our health is also buoyant like a cork.

ASK: If we hold a cork under water, and then let go, what happens?

[this should be obvious]

It pops up to the surface.

That's the same thing that this kind of thinking does to our innate health. It holds it down so we can't see it. But as soon as this thinking lets go, it pops up to the surface, just like Mr./Ms. Cool.

We don't have to do anything to find our health. It is always there. It will pop up naturally if that thinking stops for a moment.

The path is a calm mind or a clear head. In that state, our heath, our healthy thinking, our wisdom reveals itself to us — and it's available to us at any time, any time our head clears or calms.

We're only one thought away from our health at any time. Anybody is! Is that hopeful or what?!

We just don't know when that one thought is going to appear. But clear head makes it more likely to happen.

That's how it all works.

Simple, isn't it? But awesome! Adults make things so complicated.

ASK: What does "infinity" mean?

[entertain ideas]

It means never ending.

We create infinite kinds of thoughts and bring them to the surface in our heads. Some of these point us toward our health and some point us away from it. Some can be real nice; some can be downright tortuous and painful.

ASK: Why do you think we sometimes torture ourselves with certain thoughts, when we can call to mind any kind of thoughts?

[entertain ideas]

Because of those thought habits.

A thought habit can be broken when we realize it isn't good for us to keep recycling it.

[ask the class if they understand what this means, and emphasize it]

Remember, as we discussed in a previous session, the opposite of filling our heads with these thought habits is a clear mind.

We all get affected by what is on our minds. We affect other people by acting out what is on our minds.

ASK: When do you feel most in control of yourself and your life? Why?

[brief discussion]

When we go to the higher [or deeper] levels where thought is very quiet, it is like a library in a big mansion. We have direct access to a lot of wisdom and common sense. The thoughts we generate there are calmer, more relaxed, more spontaneous. The thoughts are fresh, pure and uncontaminated by what others have told us or what we have made up about life in a bad moment.

ASK: Can anyone here describe what a clear mind feels like? Everybody really knows — even if you've only had the experience for a moment or two.

[entertain ideas]

Yes! And it feels safe, like we're less likely to make mistakes and get people mad when we're in a clear head. We're actually more intelligent.

All that stuff we've heard about clearing our heads before a test makes sense. That's why it's suggested to not cram at the last minute. We want a clear head going into a test, where we have access to much more than what we think we "know." We can trust ourselves and our judgment when our heads are clear.

ASK: Raise your hands if you are sold on the merits of a clear head; that is, if you think it's a valuable thing to have.

[Ask anyone who raised their hands if they are willing to try to tell others why it's so good for them. If that doesn't work, drop it. If everyone raised their hands, move on.]

Okay, for those who are sold on a clear mind, you may be wondering, "Okay, it's important, but how do you do it?"

Here is what will help:

1. We have to know it is valuable for us to clear our heads. We have to see the merits of it and respect it.

2. We have to not want to fuel all those negative thoughts that get in our way, and when they come up we need to recognize them as thoughts that are not doing us any good.

3. If that doesn't work, we can try to distract our busy minds by doing something that will hold our interest long enough to drop the old thoughts. We already do that now, perhaps without realizing it. For some people, listening to music does it, so long as they don't start relating the words back to their problem. For other people other things do it for them.

ASK: What other things do you do that can distract your mind from unproductive thinking?

[list on board]

TASK: [get everyone in a quiet feeling, and speak slowly, in a soft voice] Everyone close your eyes and relax. ~ Slowly, take two or three deep breaths ~ and just let your mind and your body completely relax. ~ Imagine this: You wake up one day and you feel like a completely new and renewed human being. Something is very different and you don't know what it could be, but you do know one thing — you feel SO good, SO peaceful, like you've been kissed by angels during your sleep. You can't even bother wondering about what has happened. You just want to savor it as long as it will last. ~ You go about your usual morning routine, but it all seems so different to you. You feel touched by things that used to seem so ordinary. ~ As you turn the sink faucet on you are aware of the miracle of water and how fortunate you are to live in a time and place that water is so easy to come by. You only have to turn the faucet! ~ You notice the beams of light streaming in your window and the distant, sweet sound of a bird. ~ As you get in the shower you wonder why you never noticed how soothing it feels on your skin. ~ As you eat breakfast you notice how breakfast tastes SO great!

It's the same breakfast you always eat, but it's as though you're tasting it for the first time. ~ Just be with that feeling for a few minutes and see everything in the world with these "new eyes." ~ ~ ~

[after a few moments, say something like —] What could be happening to you? The world hasn't changed. What do you think is going on? But don't answer this out loud — just reflect on it for yourselves.

[gently bring them back to the room]

ASK: Write down your thoughts about what could be happening to you.

[give them a few minutes to do this]

ASK: Would anyone be willing to share their ideas?

[discussion]

Our thinking shut down enough so that our thoughts became so quiet that it allowed our deeper feelings to transform our "normal" experience and transcend our usual programmed response to life. "Transcend" means, "to rise above" or to "pass beyond." "Transform" means "to change the form of." We are going beyond what we normally see. We are seeing from a higher perspective.

F. Home Practice

Make a point of noticing when you slip into a clear mind when your thoughts are quiet. Just take note of the quiet feeling of inner peace and security. Savor it while it lasts. Be grateful for it. Notice any wise thoughts or insights or solutions to a question that you've had that might come to mind. You will recognize that such thoughts come from a deeper place because of their freshness. These ideas are original and new. If it's an old thought that you've had before, then you've slipped back into process thinking. Such is life. What will be, will be. Don't fret. But when you get the chance, write down what thoughts popped into your head from out of the blue. Write down whether they gave you a solution to something, or an insight.

Feel the difference between your usual process-computer thinking and free-flowing-receiver thinking. Feel what it's like to have a clear head!

G. Summary/Conclusions

Healthy mental functioning looks and feels like this:

a) when we are in a peaceful, serene state of mind in the absence of heavy or busy or stressful thinking;

b) when we are thinking low-quality thoughts but recognize that we are thinking in unhealthy, unproductive ways and that it is only temporary and we don't have to take it too seriously;

c) when we know that the pathway to healthy functioning is through a clear head which gives us access to our inner health and wisdom.

We hope that students will have gained insights into how valuable a relaxed state of mind is, and into how they are naturally motivated and more creative in a calm state of mind. People are sometimes reluctant to quiet their minds, thinking they'll become lazy. Not so! People are lazy only if their minds are full of thoughts such as, "I've got too much to do. I'm over-whelmed," or "I'm not good enough," or, "I'll mess things up," or, "I'm not interested." People are generally more productive when their minds are free and clear.

diagram 1:
Innate Health

Self-Esteem
Natural Deep Feelings
INNATE HEALTH
Peace of   Wisdom
Mind
Mental   Common
Health   Sense

diagram 2:
Innate Health and The Thinking That Obscures It

THOUGHTS THAT TAKE US
AWAY FROM OUR HEALTH

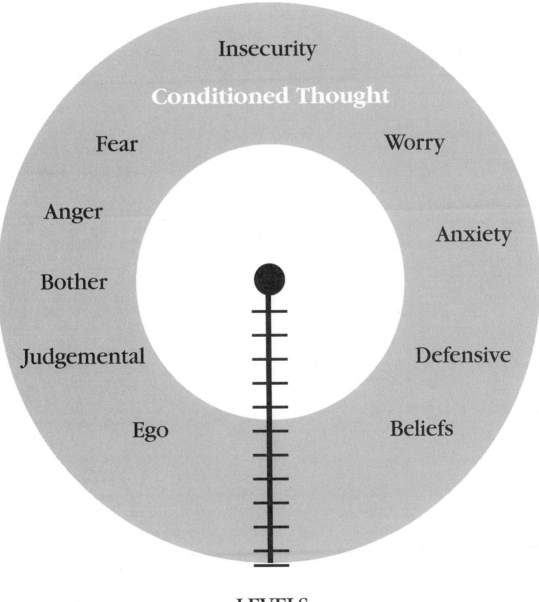

Insecurity

Conditioned Thought

Fear

Worry

Anger

Anxiety

Bother

Judgemental

Defensive

Ego

Beliefs

LEVELS

diagram 3:
Innate Health and The Thinking That Obscures It

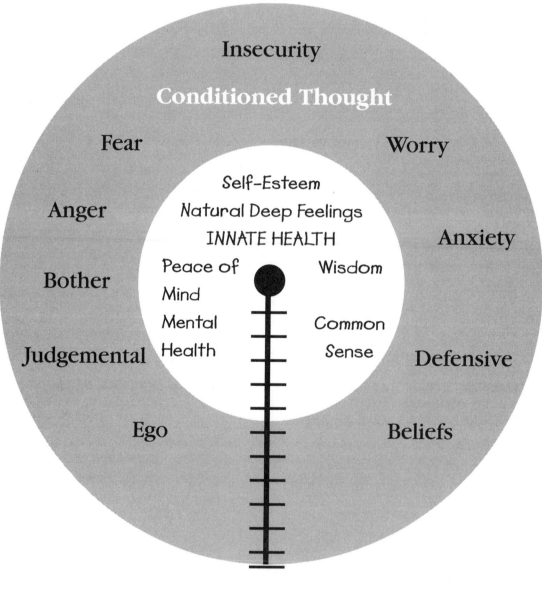

THOUGHTS THAT TAKE US
AWAY FROM OUR HEALTH

Insecurity

Conditioned Thought

Fear   Worry

Self-Esteem
Anger   Natural Deep Feelings
                   INNATE HEALTH   Anxiety

Bother   Peace of   Wisdom
             Mind
             Mental   Common
Judgemental Health   Sense   Defensive

Ego   Beliefs

LEVELS

Session Fourteen

Self-Esteem vs. Self-Image

A. To Teachers

Self-esteem arises naturally from that healthy, inner place inside us. When we are not entertaining low quality thoughts about ourselves, we have perfect self-esteem. Our self-image, on the other hand, comes from the way we have come to think about ourselves. This may not be in accord with our natural self-esteem. Which will we believe?

The only thing that can possibly interfere with our natural self-esteem is thinking that creates a different image of ourselves.

This session presents a different than usual view of self-esteem. Again, society has looked to the outside world for answers to self-esteem, instead of to where it originates — inside each of us. If we observe people who we would say have high self-esteem, we would see that they do not judge themselves. In other words, they do not go out of their way to think positive thoughts about themselves. They do not wonder if they have self-esteem. They just go about their life generally satisfied and do not take their lows too seriously. The answer to self-esteem, then, is not to think highly of ourselves; rather, it is not to judge ourselves at all. When we do not judge ourselves our natural state will rise to the surface and take over.

To put it another way, if self esteem is already there for us naturally, we do not have to do anything to ourselves to attain it — because we already have it. Because it is already in us naturally we need not go out of our way to give ourselves good messages. In fact, to give ourselves good messages only distracts us from feeling our self-esteem naturally. Contrary to popular opinion (in some circles), this means that "affirmations" are unnecessary and could even get in the way because they inadvertently may carry with them automatic doubt. In other words, deep down, we know we wouldn't have to give ourselves affirmations if we felt good about ourselves. We can't really fool ourselves.

This is why a lot of self-esteem programs in schools defeat their own purpose by teaching students to think good thoughts about themselves. Sure, it is better than thinking negative thoughts about themselves, but it takes so much effort to think positive thoughts if students don't really believe it about themselves. Another drawback is that affirmations inadvertently set up comparisons. For example, we may be doing well now, but will we be later? We may be doing well now, but how well compared to the next person? On the other hand, if we do not question ourselves or how well we're doing, we automatically have self-esteem. Thus, we can only think ourselves away from it.

In summary, but for negative thinking about ourselves, self-esteem is there for us naturally and automatically.

Self-Esteem vs. Self-Image

B. Key Points

◆ Self-esteem is automatic, from that natural, healthy place within.

◆ We also carry an image or concept of ourselves that may not feel like we have self-esteem, but it is only a set of thoughts, and we decide which we let guide us.

◆ The only thing that can get in the way of natural self-esteem is our thoughts about it, so the less we think about or evaluate ourselves the more our natural self-esteem takes over.

Sample Questions for Reflective Discussion

What do you think is the difference between self-esteem and self-image?

If we are born with natural self-esteem that never goes away, how do we forget that we have it?

Do you feel better when you're not thinking about yourself or when you're thinking about how well you're doing?

How do you think you get more self-esteem?

C. Needed Materials

Overhead/chart: "Self-esteem vs. Self-image" [found at end of chapter]

Overhead/chart: "You're on the free throw line . . ." [found at end of chapter]

D. Opening Statement

In your home practice, did anyone have any insights when your head cleared, or did you have any insights about the importance of keeping your head clear?

[discussion]

Today we're going to talk about self-esteem and what it is, and the difference between self-esteem and the image we have of ourselves. When talking about it, you will see that it sums up many of the things we've covered so far.

E. Activity/Story Line

ASK: What is self-esteem?

[briefly entertain ideas]

Self-esteem is really just generally feeling pretty good. That's all it is.

ASK: Where does self-esteem come from?

This is where most people make a mistake. People think they get their self-esteem by the way other people treat them. But that's not really the way it works.

Here is a story about it:

Once there was a girl with very, very long hair. Every night she went to sleep and snuggled in and slept very peacefully. One day as she was walking along the street she met someone who asked, "I hope you don't mind my asking you this, but I used to have very long hair like yours, and I used to sleep with my hair on top of the blankets, and I was always curious whether other people with long hair slept with their hair over or under the blankets. The girl thought for a moment and said, "Gee, I never thought about it before. I don't really know what I do. Sorry, I can't help you."

That night when the girl was going to sleep, she found herself with her hair under the blankets. She thought, "Hey, I guess I sleep with my hair under the blankets. If I see that person again, I'm going to have to tell her that I sleep with my hair under the blankets."

The girl closed her eyes to go to sleep, and then she thought, "I wonder what it would be like to sleep with my hair over the blankets. So she put her hair over the blankets. "Hmmm," she thought, "my neck gets a little chilly out here." So she put her hair back under the blankets?. "Hmmm," she thought, "but this feels like it tugs a little under here." So she pulled her hair out. "Yeah, this feels a little more free. Gee, I wonder if I really do sleep with my hair under the blankets after all. Neither one really feels all that comfortable."

That was the last peaceful night's sleep that girl had (until she gave up and cut her hair short). For the rest of her long-haired life she had the issue in her head of where to put her hair when she slept.

This is an example of what we do to ourselves. When we're not thinking about something, it's not a problem for us. It's only when we start thinking about it or worrying about it that it becomes a problem.

It's the same way with self-esteem. When we're not thinking about whether we feel good about ourselves or not, it's not a problem. It only becomes a problem — we only wonder whether we have it — when we think about it, when it's on our mind.

Otherwise it's natural. We just have it.

How do we know this?

This goes back to what we were talking about earlier in these sessions: We automatically have self-esteem. When little babies come into the world they don't have self-esteem problems. They are just filled with wonder, except when they feel uncomfortable. Otherwise, they are pure joy.

That wonder, that pure joy, then, is natural. And it never goes away. We only forget that we have it and, when we forget, we think we no longer have it.

True self-esteem is a feeling of well-being that doesn't depend on any particular thoughts. It is just feeling good about life and everything in it.

ASK: Who can take our self-esteem away from us?

[briefly entertain ideas]

No one! Parents can do all kinds of bad things to kids and the kids' thinking gets messed up. Teachers can do the same. But the only thing that can get in the way of people's self-esteem is their own doubts about it, their own thoughts about it.

Suppose you're on the high school basketball team. If you win this game you win your league's championship. Your team is up by one point but with seven seconds left to play, the other team scores a basket and now they are up by one point. Your team has no time outs left. Your team quickly puts the ball in play and races up the court. Your best player shoots with two seconds on the clock. The other team blocks the ball and it ends up in your hands. In reflex, you shoot — but you're fouled, just as the buzzer goes off to end the game.

You have two free throws. Your team is down by one point. All eyes are on you. If you make the free throws, your team wins the game and the championship. If you miss even one, it's all over. You're on the line. Everyone has left the floor because there is no time left on the clock.

ASK: What might you say to yourself at this point?

[entertain ideas]

[After the students have responded, write the following on the board one at a time, but write the lowest one first, from the bottom up, as you did in the "levels of understanding" section. The way it appears below is the way it will finally appear on the board:]

- ◆   Clear the head. Say nothing. Total focus on the ball and the basket.

- ◆   "You're good enough to do this. You can do it!"

- ◆   "Okay, you can do this if you just follow the right process: Get balanced. Eyes on the rim. Elbow straight. Follow through."

- ◆   "Oh Geez, I wonder if I can do this!"

- ◆   "Oh no! Why me?! I'll never be able to do this. I'm not good enough."

Which one do you think will have the best chance of getting the ball in the basket?

Obviously, if you're thinking low thoughts about yourself, the odds of the ball going in the basket are very low. Nothing is going to work right if those are the thoughts you're giving yourself. The best cheerleader in the world couldn't drown out those loud messages in your head.

If you question whether you can do it, just by the mere question you're putting doubt into your mind, and you're not much better off than the person thinking low thoughts.

If you tell yourself you can do it if you just follow the technique well enough, you're filling your mind with too much clutter to be able to focus enough.

If you're giving yourself affirmations or trying to think positive to give yourself confidence that you can do it, there still might be something way in the back of your mind that tells you, "Hey, you wouldn't have to be standing here saying this stuff to yourself if you really were confident about this."

If you don't question it at all, if the focus is directed at the right place without any distractions, you probably have the best chance of getting it in. That's what Michael Jordan does.

It is the exact same thing with self-esteem:

As long as you think badly of yourself, you'll never find it.

If you wonder how well you're doing, you'll produce doubt.

If you try to follow techniques, you'll clutter your mind.

If you try to give yourself confidence through affirmations or positive thinking such as "I'm good looking," you'll be closer but you'll still wonder why you have to be saying this to yourself if you really had self-esteem.

If you don't think about yourself, you'll automatically have it. It's there automatically anyway, deep down inside, and it only goes away when we start questioning it or thinking ourselves away from it.

People who have high self-esteem never think about it.

ASK: Think of someone you know who you would say has high self-esteem. What makes you think they have it? Have you ever seen them talk to themselves about it? Do you think they think about it?

[Break the class into groups of three to talk about it. Give them about 10 minutes]

ASK: What do you think you can do to get more self-esteem?

[entertain ideas]

Forget about it! Just live life and put your whole heart and soul into what you're doing at the moment. Just accept the good feeling of doing your best. Just be a good friend, or help someone out. Just enjoy. Then it will be there automatically.

And if you find the question about whether you're good enough or worthy enough coming back into your mind, just chalk it up to one of those crazy thoughts that we all get and don't pay it any mind. It flew into your head; let it fly right out again. To hold it in your head is to take it seriously. We do not want to take thoughts like that seriously.

And here's a little secret: If any of you grew up in a family where you were always treated badly, or were always told how worthless you were, and that has caused a lot of thoughts about yourself that are pretty low, just remember: you think those low thoughts about yourself because you took to heart what they said about you — with good reason, probably — but no one, no matter what they do to you or say to you, can ever take away the naturally healthy self-esteem inside you, because it is indestructible. It's impossible! Because that's what you really are. The only way it can be taken away is for you to believe what they said, and to think that it's true. It's not!

We are who we are — we are that natural healthy self, deep down inside — no matter what we think of ourselves. Everything else is an illusion. It's a trick.

If we find ourselves having a low opinion of ourselves, it's either because we picked up a habit of thinking that makes us see it that way, or we've dropped into a low mood. In either case, we can ignore or dismiss that thinking.

Low self-esteem is only present at the exact moment we're thinking bad thoughts of ourselves. At the very next moment those thoughts can pass, as soon as we get involved or engrossed in something. At those moments our low self-esteem goes away — until we think those thoughts the next time. It is a moment-to-moment state.

ASK: If you and your friends had low self-esteem, and all of a sudden there was a fire in the school, and in trying to get out you found the door locked, and you all had to get out of there, do you think anyone would have low self-esteem right then?

[discussion]

You have low self-esteem only when you have time to think those thoughts. High self-esteem is your natural state. You are the only one who can create low self esteem — through your own thoughts and beliefs about yourself.

[Go over the self-esteem vs. self-image chart, to be sure the students understand the difference between self-esteem and self-image.]

F. Home Practice

When you go about your business at home or with your friends, if you start having any low thoughts about yourself, dismiss them as irrelevant or unneeded or meaningless thoughts. Do this for as long and as often as you can.

G. Summary

Ideally, students would walk away with an insight, something like: "No matter how I feel about myself at any given time, and no matter what anyone tells me about myself, no one can take my inner good feelings away from me. I am the only one who can take it away — with my own temporary, off-the-mark thinking."

SELF-ESTEEM VS. SELF-IMAGE

Self-esteem	Self-image
◆ a general feeling of well-being	◆ thinking whether we feel good about ourselves or not
◆ what we are inside	◆ what we think about ourselves
◆ naturally present in us	◆ we have to *think* it
◆ not actively thinking about ourselves	◆ actively thinking about ourselves
◆ can't be destroyed	◆ comes and goes with our thinking

You're on the free throw line on the last second of a crucial game with the score tied. What might you say to yourself, and which would be most effective?

- ◆ Clear the head. Say nothing.
  Total focus on the ball and the basket.

- ◆ "You're good enough to do this. You can do it!"

- ◆ "Okay, you can do this if you just follow the right
  process: Get balanced. Eyes on the rim.
  Elbow straight. Follow through."

- ◆ "Oh Geez, I wonder if I can do this!"

- ◆ "Oh no! Why me?! I'll never be able to do this.
  I'm not good enough."

Session Fifteen

Emotional Reactions:
What To Do With Thoughts We Don't Want

A. To Teachers

When you think of an emotional reaction, do you think of a scene in your classroom when World War III seemed to erupt out of nowhere and your classroom suddenly looks like a melodrama playing on your least favorite soap opera?

No matter who the players are the process that it sets off seems like a time bomb. It goes like this: something happens. You have a thought about what just happened. That thought conjures up all kinds of horrible images (probably from the past). Our imagination then comes into play and we get frightened of what might be. We react, and then the explosion occurs. That is what an emotional reaction looks like in slow motion.

Until we understand the composition of an emotional reaction, we are like silly putty — totally at the service of our emotions, with nowhere to go. Once we understand, we don't have to fall prey to those emotions. We can see the reaction coming and know that we are really making up the imagery and the reaction in our own heads. Our reaction is not "life." When we think that the reaction is "reality" — in other words, given the situation, we have no choice but to react that way — we react as if it is reality.

Yet, when we understand our reaction for what it is, we become somewhat removed from it. It is like looking at a tornado on a TV screen in the safety of our own living rooms, as opposed to being in the storm.

Emotional reactions come from thoughts. Remember, we said that all thoughts ultimately are our own illusions of reality. We have the choice whether to drop our reaction to the illusion (or the other's reaction), or to play it out.

We only don't have the choice when we do not see it. In that case, we just react. Seeing what is going on is the key.

Some folks believe that strong emotional reactions are good because they fuel action. For example, if we get upset enough at how the environment is being treated we will get off the couch and do something about it. Not so! Lots of people get that upset and stay on the couch and complain about it. Other people in good spirits believe that it is morally right to protect the environment, so they take it upon themselves — without the upset or anger — to do something about it.

Many times when we are enjoying life we have a natural interest and curiosity. There are too many interesting, enjoyable things to do to even think about spending our lives on the couch. Emotional reactions can be so exhausting that we could wind up on the couch out of sheer exhaustion and then fool ourselves into thinking that it will take another emotional reaction to get us going again.

The past, although very real when it happened, is now only a memory carried through time via our thoughts. When that memory gets triggered, we get an emotional reaction. When we do, we are at a fork in the road. The path we go down will determine whether the emotional reaction will be a passing thought, or whether it will become part of our life. We can explore its details and go back into our past to try to figure out where it came from, or we can remind ourselves that some reaction has been triggered, and it means our thoughts are tricking us and making us feel insecure, so we can't take them too seriously. Each path is a different reality that we choose. We have it in our power — it is possible — and we have the free will to drop the thought from our memory (and if we can't seem to drop it, we can at least realize what we are doing to ourselves — and discredit it). It's a choice we make.

B. Key Points

◆ Bad things may have happened to us in the past, but although very real and terrible when they happened, now they are only memories carried through time by our thoughts.

◆ When these kinds of memories pop into our heads, we get an emotional reaction, and then we decide whether we allow it to be a passing thought — just something that has been triggered — or whether it will be our life.

Sample Questions for Reflective Discussion

Why do you think people react emotionally (yell, throw a fit, fight, etc.) at times?

What kinds of things do you tend to get emotional reactions about?

If not everyone gets emotional reactions about the same things or in the same kinds of ways, where do you think these emotional reactions come from?

What do you think is the healthiest way to deal with emotional reactions when you have them?

C. Needed Materials

paper and pen or pencil

written instructions for activity (skit), either posted or written on the board, or handed out

overhead or drawing of emotional reaction fork in the road

D. Opening Statement

ASK: Did anyone find out anything interesting about not thinking about yourself?

[Brief discussion, but if no one says anything, say something like, "Good, let's not even think about our self-esteem today. Thinking about our self-esteem isn't good for us. It's just there, unless we think ourselves out of it. Let's move right on.]

In this session we are going to be talking about emotional reactions.

Imagine this: you're walking down the road minding your own business and suddenly — boom! — some terrible thought fills your head and out of nowhere you have an emotional reaction. You might get afraid or angry or jealous or some other emotion. Or perhaps, some kid comes up to you after school and tells you something that someone else said about you. The kid walks away and you find yourself continuing a dialogue in your head, "What right did he have to say that?" "How could she have said that about me!" "What business is it of his?" "Am I really like that?" "Is that what people really think of me?" "That jerk. I can't believe he had the nerve to say that to me!" The bad feeling builds and you start imagining how you'll get revenge or you get so bummed out that you can't concentrate on anything you're supposed to do.

E. Activity/Story Line

ASK: What is an emotional reaction? Any ideas?

[brief discussion]

An emotional reaction is simply some emotion that we feel that gets triggered by something or someone. What really gets triggered is our thoughts, and then it causes us to feel those emotions.

ASK: Where do these thoughts that trigger our emotions come from?

[discussion]

Mostly from our memories. We all have memories. Everything that ever happens to us gets stored in our memories. They all get stored in our heads. They don't cause us any problems unless those memories get triggered by something — and then we get a reaction. So the thoughts we have in our heads cause our emotional reactions.

Also, as we have seen, sometimes the way we see things causes us to react to something that other people would not react to — and vice-versa.

ASK: What can we do about these reactions when we have them?

[discussion]

The first thing to know is that there is not much we can do about having emotional reactions. Everyone has their own things that they react to.

What we can do when we have them is to let them come in and give us whatever reaction they give and say to ourselves something like, "Whoa, where did that reaction come from?!" The answer is, some memory just got triggered, and it doesn't really mean anything. We're back at the fork in the road. The reaction blew into our head; we can either let it blow out again, or we can take it to heart and dwell on it.

TASK: On a piece of paper, write down briefly what some things are that you might have had emotional reactions about. What gets to you — in one way or another?

[give them a few minutes for this]

TASK: Now get into groups of six or so. Your job is to create a little skit or play, based upon any one (or more) of the reactions that people in your group wrote down.

Here is what you have to do as part of your play:

[it would be best if these instructions were posted or written out]

1) Come up with something that sets off or triggers the reaction.

2) Come up with what someone would have been thinking before they had the reaction.

3) Come up with what someone might have done once they had the reaction that would get them into trouble.

4) Then come up with another possible ending where the person could have handled the reaction in a healthier way. In other words, think of what other thoughts someone could have had to have a different ending.

[give them about 15 or 20 minutes to come up with a skit]

[come back to the full group and have each small group run their skits — first with one ending, then the other. If time permits and you have access to a video camera you might videotape their skits.]

ASK: What made the endings different? Were the results different?

[discussion]

We have the power to stop how far we let the reaction drag us down at any point. When we can recognize what is happening we will instantly regain our perspective. Then we will have full power to choose between going downhill carrying the emotional reaction further, or choosing to act from a higher perspective. When we are in the middle it seems like there is no choice. But when we see ourselves having the reaction, and when we know where it came from — that we are reacting because of what is in our memory — we see that we most certainly have a choice about how far down it brings us. In other words, the more perspective we have, the less we are affected by that downward thinking.

[display the drawing or overhead of the emotional reaction fork in the road]

When we walk down the road and we get a reaction triggered in us, we have two choices. We can either blame our feelings on the circumstances, and then as long as those circumstances are present our reaction will either stay the same or get worse — or we can take responsibility for having the reaction. We can say to ourselves, "This reaction is coming from my own thinking!" In that case the reaction will tend to die down or go away altogether. We get to decide which fork we walk down.

F. Home Practice

Notice whether you have any emotional reactions and consider your two possible endings, like in the skits.

G. Summary

Ideally we want students to be saying, "If I get an emotional reaction, that doesn't mean I have to let it bring me down. I can see the source of the reaction as my own thinking (as opposed to being caused by the situation), and it will pass if I let it go. In fact, as soon as I realize that I've been caught in an emotional reaction, I can stop myself and begin to back away from it. However, I'm helpless until I recognize it."

Emotional Reactions Crossroads

emotion
gets weaker

my own thinking is
causing this

at Crossroads

anger/fear/worry

that person (or situation)
is causing this

emotion stays the same
or gets stronger

Session Sixteen

Insecurity And Fear

A. To Teachers

In previous sessions we talked about how insecurity and fear lies at the root of all problem behaviors, as well as anger, depression, jealousy, guilt, hurt feelings, and so forth.

How do we know this?

We can see how it plays out in day-to-day life. Our child is an hour late from an agreed-to curfew. We are petrified that something horrible has happened to her. She finally walks in. We are on her like an attack dog.

In a relationship, we can look at the beginning and the end of a "fight." At the beginning the couple is embroiled in anger. After the dust has settled and the parties have regained their composure and perspective, insecurities are often uncovered. We can hear it in the apology: "I'm sorry I reacted like I did. I was afraid that you weren't considering my needs enough." "I'm sorry I overreacted. I was scared that I wasn't attractive to you anymore." "I'm sorry I came down on you about your eating habits. I'm just afraid that you're putting your life in jeopardy."

Insecurity or fear are at the root of all our emotions.

Yet, we have another set of natural, deeper feelings, such as compassion, humility, gratitude, humor. If we were not thinking insecure or fearful thoughts we would automatically feel the deeper feelings.

Behind all "bad" or troublesome behaviors in our classrooms lies insecurity or fear. The behavior problem is usually not what we think it is. The problem, really, is insecurity. The way to solve the behavior problem is to get to the root of the insecurity. Remember, the root of the insecurity is insecure thinking that the troublesome student does not know about. That student would be helped by understanding what insecurity is, and how it gets people to do things that they wouldn't do if they had their wits about them. That is what this session (and this entire curriculum) hopes to accomplish.

B. Key Points

◆ Underneath anger, depression, hurt, jealousy, guilt, blame, acting out, etc. lie thoughts of insecurity and fear that fuel the emotions and keep us from seeing with perspective.

◆ When people recognize where their emotions are coming from and how they often compel us to act in troublesome or troubled ways, they are less likely to buy into those emotions and let them run their lives.

Sample Questions for Reflective Discussion

What do you think creates insecurity and fear? What kinds of thoughts do you think lie behind anger, desperation, jealousy, guilt, blame, and acting out?

If someone was doing something that really bothered you, what do you think the difference would be in how you reacted toward them if you saw them as insecure, or if you saw them as troubling or out to get you?

C. Needed Materials

paper and pencil or pen

D. Opening Statement

ASK: What did you notice about your emotional reactions?

[discussion]

In this session we will look further at emotional reactions and what lies behind them. We will talk about how fear and insecurity can sometimes rule our lives without our knowing it.

E. Activity/Story Line

During school vacation, Donna went to the mall and saw her boyfriend, James, standing there talking with a very pretty girl, Keisha. Donna ducked behind a corner so he wouldn't see her. She peeked. James's face was all smiles. Donna ran out of the mall filled with jealousy. For the next week she was depressed and couldn't even speak with him when he called. The next time she saw James at school she was so angry that she slapped him in the face.

ASK: Where do you think Donna's emotions of jealousy, then depression, then anger came from?

[discussion]

It all gets back to insecure or fearful thoughts.

ASK: What are some things that Donna might have been insecure or fearful about?

[list their responses on the board]

Examples:

- insecure that she wasn't as pretty as Keisha

- afraid that she would lose her boyfriend

- afraid that she'd be alone

TASK: Think of a time when you felt jealous, depressed or angry — or worried, or anxious, or when you wanted to blame someone or something else for a mistake you made. (Use a different situation than you did for the last session.) Reflect on whether your emotions may have had any insecurity or fear behind them. On a piece of paper 1) write down the situation, 2) write down what your emotions were, and 3) write down whether you can find any insecurity or fear behind those emotions. Do not put your names on these papers. I will be collecting them and shuffling them together and will pick a few to read to the class

[Give them a few minutes to do this, then collect and shuffle them and have a student blindly pick one that you then read.]

TASK: Your job is to see whether you can be detectives and uncover what might be the fear or insecurity behind the emotion.

[discussion]

**[Then move on to the next one.
Repeat this process with at least three of the papers.]**

ASK: Now, do you think that anything lies behind the fear and insecurity?

[entertain ideas. If they say "thought," say something like "Great! What kind of thought?" If they say "thoughts of fear or insecurity" say something like "Great! Where do those thoughts come from?"]

[write on the board] "Fear and insecurity = memory + imagination."

Fear and insecurity are really "memory" plus "imagination." Let's see how this works.

Let's say that when we were little children we got stung by a bee, or one of our friends told us how much it hurt when he got stung, or we saw a TV program where people got attacked by a swarm of bees. That gets stored in our memory.

Then, some time we're outside playing, and a bee flies by our head. Our memory kicks in. We remember about how much the bee sting hurt (or might hurt).

Then, our imagination kicks in. We imagine what it would be like to be stung, and we freak out. We get scared and full of fear over this bee. But our fear is really only our memory plus our imagination at work.

It's the same with all fear.

Let's say you were going out with someone and you fell in love and really started to get involved in this relationship, and then the person left for someone else, or was suddenly mean to you. That gets put in our memory. Then, over time, we see someone else that we could really be interested in, and we want to get involved — but something stops us.

Our memory kicks in about how much the last relationship hurt when it ended. Then our imagination kicks in. "What if I throw myself into this relationship and then she leaves me and I'm left with all that pain again? I don't know if I can take it!?" So we get scared and think, "I'd better not get that involved with someone again so I won't be hurt."

The thing is, all that thinking in our head happens so fast that we don't even realize that we're thinking at all. It goes by us like lightning. All we are left with is an uncomfortable feeling.

That is insecurity and fear at work — because it is memory plus imagination at work.

So, if we know what fear and insecurity is — that it is just our memory plus our imagination playing tricks on us — the next time we feel fear or insecurity, at least we can know what is really going on.

But it gets even more complicated. The problem is, we pick up that memory through our senses. For example, if we see a scary horror movie, we actually feel it — so we get frightened. Sometimes we can even feel our skin tingle, or we can feel our stomachs tighten. We are having a "real" experience of fear — even though it is only on a movie screen.

It's the same with our memory. If we have scary thoughts in our memory, we actually feel scared. Sometimes we can feel our skin tingle or feel our stomachs get tight.

But it is only our thoughts taking our memory and playing with it through our imagination. That is what gives us those scary feelings.

Now, if we know this, the next time we get scared about something, if we know where it is coming from, maybe it won't get to us so much. All we have to do is keep realizing it. Sometimes this is not so easy, but only because our memory and imagination don't want to let go. This is what Slick does to us.

On the other hand, Cool tells us to watch out when we need to be careful. Cool would tell us not to go walking down a dark alley at night in a neighborhood where people have gotten mugged. Cool gives us that wisdom and common sense. But that's different from the fear we get from Slick playing with our memory and imagination.

Insecurity or fear is like a seed from a plant that blows into our minds.

ASK: What makes a plant grow?

Water.

ASK: What happens to a seed when it gets water?

It starts to grow roots.

ASK: What makes a thought grow in our head?

[briefly entertain ideas]

Attention.

A thought of fear or insecurity will blow into our mind. The more we give that thought attention — the more we think about it, the more we dwell on it — the more it grows roots and stays with us. Then we have this huge thought in our head with roots that won't let go.

ASK: If a seed blows onto the ground and it doesn't get water, what happens?

It either dies, or it blows away.

ASK: If a thought of insecurity or fear blows into our heads and we don't give it attention, what happens?

It either dies, or it blows away.

ASK: What does it mean to not give the thought attention?

[discussion]

We can see it — even feel it — acknowledge that it's there — but if we know that it is just a thought that popped into our heads and it doesn't really mean anything because it is just our memory and imagination playing tricks on us, it will blow away on its own—until it pops up again later and then we can do the same thing with it.

This is a well-kept secret. Anyone who understands it will lead a healthier life.

What is the secret? To understand two little things:

1) that whenever we get angry or jealous or we want to fight or we want to act out or we get depressed or we blame others or put them down, we are really just having scared or insecure thoughts about something;

2) that fear and insecurity or any other emotion will come and go, blow into our minds and will blow out, if we do not give attention to, dwell on, react to those scary or insecure thoughts — because it is only our memory plus imagination playing tricks on us.

When we know this, and if we can notice it at the time, we keep perspective. Even if we can't notice it at the time, but we realize later what is going on, it helps us to regain perspective.

TASK: [*Hand the papers that they wrote earlier in this session back to the students. It doesn't matter whether they receive their own or someone else's.*] Pair up with someone. Your task is, given what you now know, to write a new script about what the person can do to deal with the emotions. It doesn't have to be a long one.

[*Tell the students that if any pair is having trouble coming up with a new script, you will be available to help them out.*]

[Again, collect the papers.]

ASK: What did you learn from this?

[discussion]

Remember the seed. That thought-emotion will blow in. It is based on insecurity or fear. Now that we know that, we get to decide whether we let it blow out or whether we let it grow roots in our head.

F. Home Practice

The next three times that you get upset, before blowing a gasket, answer the following: "What am I insecure or fearful about?"

Then, put each "problem" on the back burner of your mind — in other words, don't think about it — so that your deeper, free-flowing (cool) thinking can work with it. Forget about it.

As you're going about your business, write down any solutions that pop into your head from out of the blue. Remember, when you are not actively thinking about it, a cool solution will have a better chance of coming to you.

G. Summary

Insecurity or fear arise when our memory and imagination are at play. It gets worse when we buy into those fearful or insecure thoughts and make them into something by dwelling on them. Those feelings are signals to us to take heed. It means we are having low-quality, insecure thoughts. Those thoughts are misguided since they are being led by insecure thinking. "I don't want to pay attention to and follow those misguided thoughts."

Session Seventeen

Stress

A. To Teachers

Isn't it interesting that, given the same situation, we can feel completely different levels of stress than other people do? We can even feel different levels of stress ourselves in the same situation at different times. Thus, it is not the situation that causes us stress, it's what is inside our own heads.

Understanding this concept is also the solution. Often when we feel stress it is because we are taking things too personally and have lost our bearings. We think we're the victim of circumstances when it really has to do with the quality of thinking we have in that moment of time.

Often when we feel stress in our work it is because we've lost our total focus on the essence and meaning of our work. Or, we have lost sight of the task at hand in the moment, and our minds have become distracted by extraneous matters such as the past and future.

To overcome stress we must, first, take responsibility for the stress we feel. We have to admit that we are running scared. Then we have to admit that the reason we're running scared is because of our own thinking. This process leads to humility, and a calmer mind.

Everyone is vulnerable to stress because everyone has the ability to think: to evaluate, to judge, to analyze, etc. Everyone can also learn to overcome stress by understanding that the source of stress is us — not the situation — and by learning which thoughts to pay attention to and which thoughts to dismiss as irrelevant or distracting or unproductive.

A landlord once said, "I learned that I could refuse to rent space in my head to my undesirable thoughts just like I can refuse to rent an apartment to undesirable tenants!"

B. Key Points

◆ In between the situation and the stress we feel lie our own thoughts; we can either think we're the victim of circumstances or we can take ownership of the stress we feel.

◆ To overcome stress we first have to admit that we're running scared about something, then admit that the reason we're running scared is that we're not seeing things right. This makes us feel humble and calms our minds.

◆ Often when we feel stress in school or in our work it's because we've lost our focus on what we're doing in the moment, and we've become distracted by extraneous matters, such as wondering how well we or others are doing.

Sample Questions for Reflective Discussion

Why do you figure that some people get stressed about things that others don't?

Do you think that stress comes from the situation we're in or comes from our own thinking, and why?

If you feel stress how do you think you can see beyond it?

C. Needed Materials

small notepads (or a bunch of paper stapled together) and pencil or pen for interviews

overhead or drawing: Stress Particles 1 and Stress Particles 2 [found at end of session]

handout: Stress Prevention Tips [found at end of session]

handout: Stress Scale 1 and 2 [found at end of session]

D. Opening Statement

Stress is one of the biggest health problems that adults face today. It begins when they are kids.

We seem to get stressed out when we're in certain situations, such as when we're faced with a test and we don't feel prepared, or having too much to do and too little time to do it. But some people don't get as stressed out as we do, and we don't get as stressed as some other people. Even the same situation will stress us out more at some times than at other times.

ASK: Why do you think this is the case?

[discussion]

People think about those situations differently. We sometimes have different moods which means our thinking is different at different times.

[display "Stress Particles 1" overhead, or draw it on the board]

Most people think that stress comes from the situation we're in. For example, if we're in a busy city, with so much craziness going on around us, it makes sense that we'd be more stressed than someone hiking up in the peaceful mountains. We could call those little dots or lines on the picture "stress particles." It looks as if those stress particles are in the environment and surround us — to more or less of an extent.

[display "Stress Particles 2" overhead, or draw it on the board]

But this is where the stress particles really come from: our own heads. Some people who live in the crazy city are very peaceful and relaxed. Some people hiking in the mountains have minds so busy that they can't let go of all the things they think they need to do when they get back.

People either think that stress is coming from the situation, or that stress is coming from their own thinking about the situation.

Those who recognize their own thinking as the source of the stress they feel end up feeling that stress less powerfully and for a shorter time.

ASK: Let's say there's a big test coming up that is important for your final grade. What are some reasons that some people would not be stressed out?

[entertain ideas]

Some might not be stressed because they don't care. Other people really enjoy taking tests, so they are not stressed either. Still others don't feel stressed because they are totally focused on or fully absorbed in just doing it, just taking that test. They don't have time to be stressed out about it. Stress occurs when people have other things on their minds, such as being worried whether or not they will do well on the test.

The cure to stress is to clear our minds and get fully absorbed in whatever we're doing in the moment. Any thoughts about the past (that we failed some test before) or about the future (what our parents might think about how well we do) are off the task at hand and not in the moment.

E. Activity

Without disturbing anyone, you're going to go out of the classroom and find someone to interview. You're going to work with one or two others. [Note to teacher: divide up students so that those who have a tendency to disrupt or run away are paired with students who wouldn't.] Find people such as the principal, guidance counselors, the school nurse, librarian, secretaries, custodians, kitchen workers, bus drivers, anyone making deliveries to the school, or anyone in or around the school grounds. If a particular group can't find anyone, you could make a phone call to a parent or to some other adult at home or at work, but it is better to do this in person, if possible. [Note to teacher: It would be wise to tip off the school ahead of time that your students will be around doing brief interviews during this time. You may want to create a list ahead of time of possible people to interview, and have students draw names out of a hat so that all groups won't barrage the same few individuals with questions or interview requests.] Your job is to ask the person you're interviewing these questions:

[hand out these questions]

1. What gives you the most stress in your job or in other parts of your life?

2. When don't you feel stress on the job or in other parts of your life?

3. What do you think the difference is between when you feel stress or not?

4. Where do you think this stress comes from?

5. What do you do to relieve your stress?

Be back here in twenty minutes. Please be respectful of others and do not disturb anyone.

[when they return, have the pairs get into groupings of three or four to compare answers]

TASK: See if you can find any similarities or differences.

[give about five or so minutes to compare, then bring them back to the full class]

ASK: What similarities and differences did you find?

[discussion]

ASK: Let's look more specifically about what they answered for questions three and four.

[have each pair report out and make a list]

ASK: Do you think that they think that stress comes from the situation they're in or from what is inside of them?

[discussion]

ASK: Take a look at what they do to relieve their stress (question five). Do you see any relationship between where they said their stress comes from and what they do to relieve it?

[discussion]

ASK: What does this tell you about the way adults function?

[discussion]

ASK: How would you avoid being stressed out if you understood that stress begins inside your own heads?

[entertain ideas]

Here are some stress prevention tips: [give students the handout]

♦ When you feel your mind racing, and you feel like the tail is wagging the dog — take a break! (If you can't take a break, such as while taking a test, take some deep breaths and try to relax your mind.)

♦ Recognize when your thinking is unhealthy and know it's a waste of time and will get you into trouble. Know that it is not good to do the kind of thinking that causes you stress.

♦ Think only about what you are doing in the moment. We create stress by doing one thing while thinking about other things that we think we should be doing at the same time, or when we are worried or concerned about how well we or others are doing.

♦ When others do things that you end up feeling stressed about, know that it is only their insecurities or low moods talking, and don't take it personally.

♦ Don't get into other people's business.

♦ Give up being too serious. Live with an attitude of lightheartedness (while being responsible and respectful of others).

ASK: How would each of these lighten your stress?

[discussion]

[hand out the "Stress Scale"]

This scale represents where each of us lives from time to time. The terms used for each level on the scale are made up, so they are not hard and fast, but it is just a way to indicate some of the different places that we and others can be at any given time. We can be at any place along the scale at any time. We may have a tendency to generally hang around one or two of these levels more than others, but it is important to know that we are not locked in to any of these levels. We can change where we are because it is our own thinking.

[Go over each level of this scale by what is in the parentheses. If you have time, you might ask if anyone knows anyone who generally lives at each of these levels (and without using names) to describe what they're like, so students can get a better feel for each of the levels.]

◆ exhilarated or at peace

(when you feel naturally high or feel a wonderful sense of peacefulness)

◆ joyful

(when you feel great!)

◆ contented

(when you feel real nice)

◆ stressed, but generally okay

(when you're doing okay, but you're stressed out)

◆ unhappy

(when you feel down in the dumps)

◆ troubled

(when you feel that your life is out of control)

◆ tormented

(when you feel so horrible you can't move or you want to hurt others)

Anything below the line is not really healthy — even someone who is okay with the stress in his or her life. But anyone can learn to live above the line. That is what this class is about — to give people the perspective they need. That is what keeps people feeling generally free of stress.

F. Home Practice

[hand out the copy of the stress scale with the double columns]

When you notice yourself feeling stress, take the stress scale and place an "x" in the first column next to the level that best describes where you are on the stress scale at that moment. Below the scale (a) write down what is happening, what thoughts you are having, and what is your mood.

Next, find something that you can completely immerse yourself in, or completely relax. Write down what you choose to do. Go do it!

After about twenty or thirty minutes (set an alarm if you can), go back to the stress scale and in the second column place an "x" where you feel you are now on the stress scale.

Compare the two. Answer the same questions again (b).

Write down what this exercise taught you.

G. Summary

We have far more control over stress than we realize. It is easier if we catch stress early on and make up our minds to stop thinking stressful thoughts right then and there. When we are aware that we are stressing ourselves out with our own thinking, instead of it coming from some situation outside of ourselves, we are protected from the ravages of the stress.

Stress Particles 1

Stress Particles 2

Stress Prevention Tips

◆ When you feel your mind racing, and you feel like the tail is wagging the dog — take a break! (If you can't take a break, such as while taking a test, take some deep breaths and try to relax your mind.)

◆ Recognize when your thinking is unhealthy and know it's a waste of time and will get you into trouble. Know that it is not good to do the kind of thinking that causes you stress.

◆ Think only about what you are doing in the moment. We create stress by doing one thing while thinking about other things that we think we should be doing at the same time, or when we are worried or concerned about how well we or others are doing.

◆ When others do things that you end up feeling stressed about, know that it is only their insecurities or low moods talking, and don't take it personally.

◆ Don't get into other people's business.

◆ Give up being too serious. Live with an attitude of lightheartedness (while being responsible and respectful of others).

Stress Scale 1

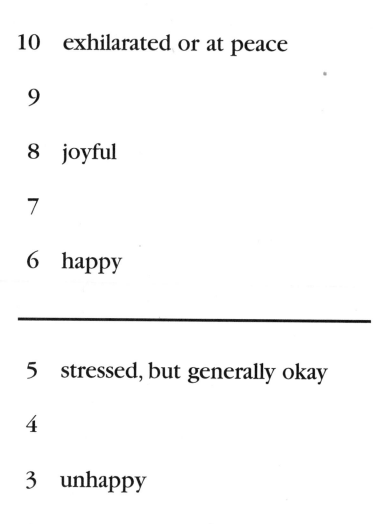

10   exhilarated or at peace

9

8   joyful

7

6   happy

---

5   stressed, but generally okay

4

3   unhappy

2

1   troubled

Stress Scale 2

	A	B
10	exhilarated or at peace	exhilarated or at peace
9		
8	joyful	joyful
7		
6	happy	happy

	A	B
5	stressed, but generally okay	stressed, but generally okay
4		
3	unhappy	unhappy
2		
1	troubled	troubled

1a. What is happening right now?

2a. What thoughts are you having now?

3a. What is your mood now?

1b. What is happening right now?

2b. What thoughts are you having now?

3b. What is your mood now?

4. **What did you learn from this activity?**

Session Eighteen
Habits

A. To Teachers

Everyone has habits. Some habits are worse than others. Some of the worst habits are those that cause people to sexually abuse or purposely harm others.

Habits stem from a feeling that drives people to do things. That feeling stems from a thought or a set of thoughts that become habitual. The behavior (smoking, biting fingernails, eating, drinking, etc.) is only the tip of the iceberg. The problem is the person walking around thinking about it all day.

A habit is several thoughts linked together without reflection. To change bad habits, the idea is to infuse reflection into the process (meaning, to look at the habit from a distance).

When we feel an urge we also have the power within us to recognize that we are having unreliable thoughts and that those thoughts will eventually pass. To break a habit we first have to see the possibility of seeing beyond it and find the "resolve" to change. We have to be honest with ourselves about how much we want to change.

Once we understand what a habit is, then, when we're feeling that way, we can make adjustments. In other words, if we are immersed in a thought habit, we can be sure that we are in computer-processing thinking. We know that this is old, recycled thinking. Because thought is nourishment for habits, we want to take our attention off the habit. The less we think about it, the better off we are.

If we are in free-flowing receptive thinking we would be generating fresh, original thoughts which are quite the opposite of a thought habit.

B. Key Points

◆ When people feel driven to do something (smoking, fighting, sexual abuse), the problem is that they go around thinking about it all day.

◆ When we feel an urge, we also have the power within us to recognize that we are having unreliable thoughts that will eventually pass.

◆ To break a habit we first have to see the possibility of seeing beyond it, be honest with ourselves about how much we would like to change, and find the "resolve" to change.

Sample Questions for Reflective Discussion

Why do people get into habits?

Think of a habit that you or somebody else has, what would you guess that the thinking looks like behind the habit?

What do you think, then, that you could do to break up the thinking and habit?

C. Needed Materials

Handout: The Process of Breaking Habits [found at end of session]

D. Opening Statement

ASK: What did you learn from placing yourself on the stress scale? What did you write down about what you learned from this activity?

[discussion]

In this session we are going to talk about something very near and dear to all of us: habits!

Everyone has thought habits.

Some people's thought habits are smoking and drinking. Other people's thought habits can be about sex. Others can be about food or being the class clown. Still others' can be about chewing pens or biting their fingernails. Others' can be swearing. Some can be about controlling others. We all have different thought habits.

ASK: Why do you think these are being called thought habits instead of just habits that we do?

[entertain ideas]

Because we have to think them before we can do them. Actually, people who do any habit feel very strongly compelled to do that habit. They feel driven to do it. But behind that feeling lies a bunch of thoughts that are making them feel that way.

We become a slave to our thought habit when we don't recognize that it's just a bunch of thoughts in the moment.

Our habits seem to control us. They control us because we think they do. If we thought differently we would not have to try to be in control of them.

E. Activity/Story Line

TASK: Select a buddy whom you know fairly well and whom you trust. Pair up.

[Note to teacher: Be sure no one feels left out of this. How you do this is up to your better judgment.]

Ask your buddy if he or she knows one of your thought habits. Both of you should do this.

[Have them take a few minutes to discuss this]

ASK: Raise your hands if you were surprised by the answer. (I'm not going to ask you what your habit is.)

Now ask your buddy whether he or she can imagine living without this habit.

[Give them a few minutes to discuss]

Now ask your buddy whether this habit gets in the way of enjoying life more. Ask if s/he would rather have this habit or stop it, and why or why not. Would s/he just kind of like to stop, or does s/he really, really want to stop, or not want to at all?

[Give them a few more minutes]

One thing is extremely important to understand. Habits usually can't be broken unless three ingredients are in place:

[show overhead or write on board or hand out handouts]

1. You've got to ADMIT that you've got a habit.

2. You've got to NOT WANT to live with the habit. In other words, you've got to think that it is not a good idea for you to have this habit.

3. You've got to KNOW you can live without this habit. In other words, you've got to see that you have it in you to be free of this habit somewhere down the road.

Those three things put us at the bus stop for breaking our habit.

Nothing can make us get on the bus —

ASK: Except what? What do you think?

[entertain ideas]

Our own thoughts! Our own thinking either puts us on the bus to break a habit or keeps us off it. It's the only thing that can make us get on or stay off.

If our thoughts are keeping our habit alive, we want to take our thoughts off the habit.

ASK: How can you help not thinking about a habit?

[entertain ideas]

Just be aware of when you are thinking those thought habits. Notice when you are thinking that way. In other words, you want to see yourself thinking those habitual thoughts. Keep being aware of when you're thinking that way. Notice how these thoughts get in the way of your being able to entertain more productive thoughts.

It may help you get on the bus, because you may find that the following process begins to happen to you naturally:

◆ Right now you're doing your habit without really being aware of it.

◆ Soon you may be doing it, and then recognizing that you're doing it.

◆ Then you may start to do it, then catch yourself.

◆ Then you may be just about to start, and catch yourself before it really starts.

◆ Then you may be just starting to think about it, and catch yourself.

◆ Finally, you find yourself not thinking about it any more.

That's when you're on the bus to break a habit.

It all happens naturally — if you keep awake about it and notice your thinking. Everyone who does this is astonished to see how often those kinds of thought habits are on our minds.

If you need help along the way, ask your buddy to help you get your mind off it.

F. Home Practice

Notice how often you get into particular thought habits.

G. Summary

You're not alone. We all have different thought habits. But we can master them by recognizing their origin in thought, and noticing them, and by catching them before they get the best of us. If we don't follow those thoughts we won't be doing the habit. If we do follow those thoughts we will be led down an alley where we would rather not be, because it's so hard to get out of.

To Break A Habit

1. ADMIT that you've got a habit.

2. NOT WANT to live with the habit. In other words, you've got to think that it is not a good idea for you to have this habit.

3. KNOW you can live without this habit. In other words, you've got to see that you have it in you to be free of this habit somewhere down the road.

4. Find the RESOLVE to break the habit. In other words, ask yourself how much you really want to break it, and be honest with yourself.

5. WATCH yourself doing the habit.

How We (Mostly) Change

◆ Right now you're doing it without really being aware of it.

◆ Soon you may be doing it, and then recognizing that you're doing it.

◆ Then you may start to do it, then catch yourself.

◆ Then you may be just about to start, and catch yourself before it really starts.

◆ Then you may be just starting to think about it, and catch yourself.

◆ Finally, you find yourself not thinking about it any more.

Session Nineteen

Learning From Mistakes

A. To Teachers

The purpose of this session is to take what we've learned thus far about thinking, and have the students apply it to problem-solving and learning from mistakes.

We would all like to be able to learn from mistakes and solve our problems, the question is, how do we do it?

Most curricula try to teach problem-solving skills or techniques. Yet, most problem-solving skills would not be necessary if people faced their problems with more perspective and common sense.

There are two ways to try to solve problems: through our processing thinking and through clear-minded insight (pop-up thinking).

In previous sessions we've discussed that when we know all the variables, process thinking is good to use, such as solving a math problem or finding our way somewhere, but process thinking is not so good for solving personal problems. Remember, Einstein said, "You can never solve a problem at the same level the problem was created," for a reason. If you knew enough to know what went wrong, you wouldn't have done it in the first place.

When we can't figure something out, and we grind away at it, we have a tendency to get upset, or down in the dumps, or frustrated. This, in turn, can lead us into a downward spiral and makes us feel more worried or insecure. When that happens we are driven more by the fear of something not happening again, rather than moving toward the best solution. We actually tend to make happen what our thinking is focused on. So if we're worried about something not happening, there is a better chance that it will happen (such as, thinking, "I hope I don't miss this ball.")

What we really need is a greater or a deeper understanding, so we can see what went wrong.

When all the variables are not known, it is better to let go of our processing, give up analyzing, clear our heads, and allow an insight to pop up from out of the blue. This will give us a higher or deeper perspective. Such answers would come from a deeper intelligence that we can only access with a clear mind. The idea in learning from our mistakes or solving our problems is to have access to it. That's what this session is about.

B. Key Points

◆ When faced with an issue or problem where all the facts aren't known, clearing the mind and allowing pop-up thinking to arise will usually give people what they need.

◆ When faced with a problem or to learn from a mistake, we can prepare our minds to receive the answers we need by admitting we don't know the answer, hoping that we will see it, trusting that an answer is there, and then forgetting about it which clears the head of it and allows an answer to pop up when we least expect it.

Sample Questions for Reflective Discussion

Do you think it's valuable to learn from mistakes? Why?

If we want to get an answer to a problem or a mistake we made that we can't seem to solve, in what way do you think we should have the best chance of getting the answer?

What is it like to have faith that an answer will come if your mind is clear enough?

C. Needed Materials

Overhead or chart on "To solve a problem — " (see end of session)

D. Opening Statement

ASK: How often did you notice your thought habits? Did any of you catch your thought habits? Did any of you start to get down on yourselves for your thought habits? If so, were you able to stop yourself and step back and just recognize it for what it is — a habit of thinking?

[discussion]

There's no sense in getting down on ourselves for thinking we can't control, because that thinking just seems to come into our heads. That's why that thinking comes to us; that's why it will probably keep coming to us. It is a habit! But we all have our own thinking habits, and those habits are different for everyone. All we have control over is what to do with them when we have them.

In this session, we're going to take this a step further.

Remember we talked about the difference between computer thinking (where Slick fills our heads with information and then processes that information) and pop-up thinking (where Cool reflects and clears the head and allows insights to pop up).

ASK: Do you remember which kind of thinking is best to use to solve math problems? Why?

[brief discussion]

ASK: Which kind of thinking do you think is best to use to solve personal problems? Why?

[brief discussion]

To review what we've talked about before, process thinking is best for doing calculations. It's best when you know all the information and you have to figure something out using what you know.

Pop-up thinking is best to use when you don't know everything that's going on, and where you want to understand everything that's involved. You might say that pop-up thinking through a clear head gets you to the heart of the matter.

ASK: Why do you think that process thinking or analyzing doesn't solve personal problems well?

[brief discussion]

It could be because you're looking through the same eyes that got you into the problem in the first place.

Analyzing what happened is looking back.

When you analyze with your computer, your mind is active and cluttered with all kinds of information. It's preoccupied.

In other words, your mind is too cluttered to see the obvious.

So you start grinding away and grinding away trying to figure out what happened, what went wrong, and you keep grinding away and grinding away, because you still only have the same information to work with, you can't possibly get anywhere. You're just working and reworking that same information, and you can't find your way out because you don't know anything new.

E. Activity/Story Line

Suppose you're faced with a problem that you don't know how to solve. Let's take a look at a situation:

Jacki was having trouble with her boyfriend, Jerry. At first everything was so nice. Jerry was so cute. They were having a great time together. She really liked being with him. But after they had been together for a while, things seemed to go bad. At first, once when they were with his group of friends, she made a remark about something, and he put her down for saying it. That really hurt. Then every once in a while he started putting her down when they were alone together. Then it started happening more often.

Jacki tried to make him happier with her. She would do anything he said. But that didn't seem to help. In fact, afterwards it just seemed to make it worse. Then Jerry broke up with her. She was crushed. He never told her why.

Jacki took her processing mind and went to work. She tried to figure out what went wrong. Why had Jerry changed? Where did she go wrong? Was she stupid? Was that why he put her down all the time? Was Jerry just a jerk when he was with his friends? But why did he even start doing it when they were alone? Maybe she went too far with him. Maybe she was unworthy. She went grinding away and grinding away.

ASK: Do you think she got anywhere? Why or why not?

[brief discussion]

ASK: What do you think she could have done instead?

**[At this point the alert students will say, "She could clear her head."
And the teacher could say, "Yes, and at the same time ..."]**

"… she could prepare herself to receive the answers she needs."

In other words, here's what she could say to herself [something like]

[Write this on the board]: "I don't have a clue what happened. I have no idea what went wrong."

Doing that relieves the mind. Saying "I don't know" frees the mind from having to know anything. It releases the mind, puts Slick out to lunch.

Then she could say [something like],

[Write on board]: "I hope to have some insight pop up that will help me see what happened, so I won't get into that same kind of problem again."

Doing that sets you up for getting the answers you need.

Then, forget about it and go about your business.

It's like playing music in a band. When you get on stage what do you need to do to play your best, or at least not make a fool of yourself up there? First, you do the preparation that you need. In this case you practice and practice over and over again so you really know the song or the piece. Then you go up there and it just comes out.

It's the same with a problem. If you do the preparation first, you cut down your chances that the problem will happen again. In this case the preparation is:

[Put up the chart found at the end of this chapter]

1. ADMIT that you're not seeing something that you need to know.

2. HOPE to see it in a new way.

Then add two more ingredients.

3. HAVE FAITH AND TRUST that you'll be able to solve it.

4. CLEAR YOUR HEAD and wait for the answer to come when you're ready.

See, here's what happens: the more you grind away at what you don't know, the more you lower your spirits, and the more you lower your spirits, the more cluttered your mind gets, and the less chance there is at getting the insights you need to solve your problems.

When you admit that you don't have a clue about what's going on here, and you hope to see it, and you trust that you will, and you clear your head, it's like running rusty water out of the pipes. All of a sudden the water is clear, and you can see what you need to see.

All that other stuff is garbage, and of no use to you.

So this is what Jacki did. She was upset for a little while, but she didn't let it drag her down. She tried to put it out of her mind, and over time she saw a new boy that she liked, and she started getting to know him, and she started going out with him, and everything was fine until one day he put her down.

Boing! Something popped into her head: "Uh oh, this is familiar. There's danger here."

See, there's something built in that protects her, if she has a clear enough mind to hear. There's something built in that protects you — if you have a quiet enough mind to hear.

So she said to him, "I want you to know that if you ever put me down again, I'm gone. I don't like it, and I won't have it!"

He didn't do it again — for a while. But then he did again, and she got that pop-up signal again and said, "Okay, I told you I won't take it, and I won't, so that's it for us." And she left.

But not before he said, "Well, you say stupid stuff sometimes, and that's why I do it."

And she said, "That's no excuse for ever putting me down. There are better ways to handle it."

Jacki was sad when she got back home, but she knew she did the right thing and was pleased with herself. She felt strong.

But a little voice was nagging at her. So she said, "I wonder if what he said about me saying stupid things was right?" So she started thinking about what she had said that he may have seen as stupid. She went back over every conversation. She started grinding away and grinding away and getting more and more agitated — until she realized what she was doing, and she said, "Wait! Stop!"

And then she said . . .

[Pull out or point to the overhead chart again while you say the following]

1. Okay, maybe I have a blind spot about saying stupid things that I don't know about. I don't have a clue about this.

2. I'd really like to find out if this is a problem for me that I'm not seeing.

3. I believe that I will see it, one way or another.

4. I'll clear my head and forget about it, just put it on the back burner and wait for something to pop up to me when I'm ready.

She forgot about it and went about her business. One day she was watching a TV program about a relationship, and the guy on the show blurted out stuff without really thinking about what he was saying, and it sounded really stupid, and it bugged her to hear it — and something popped into her head, "Hey, whoa, this is what I do sometimes. This is what bugs other people, and they don't know any better so they put me down. I still won't tolerate being put down, though, but now I know to watch what I say sometimes before I open my mouth."

Another time she did it again, but this time immediately after she did it, she knew it. Before this, she was completely unaware.

The next time, she started to say something, but realized what she was doing and caught herself.

The next time, she saw it coming, but she caught it before she opened her mouth.

Eventually she didn't even have the thought of doing it.

Jacki went on to have some really nice relationships.

That's what clearing your mind and preparing it does. It means we admit we don't know, we hope for something better, we have faith, and we put it on the back burner and stay awake for the answer when it's ready to come to us. That's our inner wisdom, our inner intelligence, our cool thoughts, speaking to us.

Then, being alert, we catch it earlier and earlier — naturally — and, after a while, it is no longer even in the cards.

ASK: Think of a situation that you have been having a problem about. How have you been trying to solve it or handle it? What might you do differently to try to solve it?

[Have the students pair up with anyone they don't mind sharing their situation with. Give them about 10 minutes. Tell them that, depending on the situation, sometimes they will want to choose their friends and at other times they will want to choose someone whom they don't know very well, and either way is okay. If some students are left over, pair them up with each other, and if any one student is left, either pair up with that student yourself or triple up one group. Have each pair decide which one would like to share their issue. The other person's job is just to listen with an open mind and if they catch anything that they don't think the other person is seeing, to offer it. But mostly you want the teller of the story to come to his or her own conclusions. Toward the end of the time the teacher can point people back to the chart. If there is time, the other person in the pair can talk about her or his issue.]

F. Home Practice

Take a look at a problem that you have or a mistake that you made that you've been thinking about (this may be the same one you shared in your pair in class, or a different one). Go through the four steps. Don't expect to get an answer right away. But notice your state of mind when you start really clearing your head and stop thinking about it — compared to when you were grinding away at it. Know that the answer will come when you're ready to hear it.

If you can't seem to let go of something, and you find yourself continuing to analyze, say (something like), "Wow, look at me grinding away at this when I know that it won't get me the answers I need. This isn't good for me. I hope I can stop thinking about this and see beyond it." And every time you catch yourself, say something like, "I can't believe I'm doing this again. It's not good for me to be doing this."

Remember, this happens to almost everyone. Don't get bent out of shape about it, just relax about it and know it's the human condition to think this way. And keep having faith that you'll get through it.

G. Summary/Conclusion

When all the information is known, use processing and analysis. When all the information is not known, use pop-up thinking, because that gets you to the heart of the matter and it gives you your answers when you least expect them, when you're not looking for the answer.

To Solve A Personal Problem

1. ADMIT that you're not seeing something right and that you don't know what to do

2. HOPE to see it in a new way

3. Have FAITH and TRUST that you'll be able to solve it

4. CLEAR YOUR HEAD and wait for the answer to come when you're ready

Session Twenty

Dealing With Hurts

A. To Teachers

It is important to know up front that this session challenges the prevailing, general understanding in the fields of counseling and prevention. At first it may not seem right; it may seem like denial. But those who keep an open mind and stick with it will open up to a world of new understandings.

At issue is what to do when we have painful memories. The generally accepted, traditional approach is that when we have such memories it is best to get down to what caused them, or express them, or get out the feelings associated with them. Many people think that it is good to keep a painful memory alive, so the same thing will not happen to them again. The problem with this is that people do not operate at full capacity when their minds are occupied by painful memories. Some people get numb, others' judgment is compromised, others see the world through a distorted lens.

Holding onto a painful memory is like poking at a bruise to make it better. Really, it only makes it hurt more.

What many people do not understand is that we have a deeper protection. It's called wisdom. With our minds clear and alert, our inner resources are available to protect us.

When people hold on to the pain of how their parents treated them, it preoccupies their minds and sets them up for misfortune because their alertness, their wisdom that is available to protect them and guide them, is hampered.

The secret is to let go, not to hold on.

B. Key Points

◆ When we feel hurts that come from painful memories, the more we hold onto those memories or the pain associated with them, the more our clear-minded wisdom is compromised.

◆ When our minds are clear, we have maximum alertness to protect ourselves, to keep ourselves safe, to have optimal responsiveness to life, and to live in a feeling of well-being.

◆ If we want to rid ourselves of hurts that we carry with us through painful memories, we can decide that it isn't good for us to carry around the pain, and let them flow through us naturally instead of stopping the flow by holding onto them.

Sample Questions for Reflective Discussion

What have you been told about how to deal with hurts that doesn't work for you? Why do you think it doesn't work?

Do you think that holding onto painful memories helps us or hurts us and why?

If something painful is happening to us in the moment, will it help us more to be upset about it, or to be angry about it, or to empty our mind, and why?

C. Needed Materials

Some container that can double as a small treasure chest. It simply needs to be able to hold up to ten pieces of paper.

Pins or tape to post papers on the wall (or you can use sticky pads, but the papers will all get stuck to each other when in the chest).

The students will need a piece of paper and something to write with.

D. Opening Statement

[Note: It will not be necessary to check in on the home practice today unless a student really wants to say something about it because today's session takes this understanding deeper.]

A football is kicked high in the air. A pass receiver waits to catch it. He has caught these high kicks hundreds of times. The last time, however, the other team had charged at him, and as soon as he caught the ball they hit him very, very hard with full force. He was nearly knocked out. He was hurt very badly.

Next time, when waiting to catch a high kick, the thought of what happened last time comes into his head. Out of the corner of his eye he sees the other team charging hard at him. He drops the ball.

The announcer says, "The poor guy heard footsteps."

Except for his memory of the last time he got creamed, he would have caught the ball easily. But his memory made him pay more attention to the footsteps bearing down on him and how much it hurt, instead of having complete focus on the ball, so he dropped it.

Memories do that to us sometimes. They take us out of our connection with the moment and put our concentration on our memories instead. We all hear "footsteps" sometimes. Our memories make us do things we wouldn't necessarily do if we had all our wits about us, such as drop footballs, act in ways that bother or hurt other people, do stupid things, or even just not do as well as we could have done otherwise.

E. Activity/Story Line

ASK: Given the memory that the football player had of getting hurt badly, and his imagination that he was going to get hurt again, is there anything that football player could have done differently in catching the ball?

[discussion]

Given his thoughts, he could not have done anything differently. He innocently dropped the ball.

The only thing he could have done differently is to have dropped his thoughts instead.

ASK: Suppose you are given a treasure map to find the secret to doing well in life. You are led from one clue to another to another to another to another, and finally you get to where the treasure is buried. You dig it up and break open the lock to the treasure chest. Inside you find a piece of paper with writing on it that contains the secret. What does it say?

Divide up into groups of five. The job of your group is to reach an agreement about what the paper says is the secret to doing well in life. When you reach an agreement, write it down on a piece of paper.

[Give the groups 10 to 15 minutes. Have each group put their paper into the treasure chest. Mix the papers around. Bring them back to the full class and ask for a volunteer to reach in and pull out one of the papers, and read it to the full class. Pin or tape it to the wall.]

ASK: Anyone from the group that came up with this one, what do you mean by this?

[entertain ideas]

ASK: What would it mean if you were to do what this says?

[discussion]

ASK: Does anyone have any other questions about what this one means for you?

[Be sure to tell them they did a great job, if they really tried to do this.]

Let's look at another one.

[Do this for each of the small groupings. At the end you have each of the group's papers pinned up on the board.]

ASK: These are great secrets. Do you think there is one right answer?

[brief discussion]

Before we say yes or no to that, let's consider some other things.

ASK: Let's say you banged your shin on a metal chair and got a bruise. After you finished putting ice on it, what would you do to make it better?

ASK: How many of you would go poking at it to make it better?

[raise hands]

ASK: How many of you would leave it alone to make it better?

[raise hands]

ASK: Let's say something bad happened to you in the past, like you got abused by someone, and it was in your memory. If that memory came up into your head and the memory hurt, how many of you would poke at it to try to make it better — in other words how many of you would try to remember it more, think about it hard, think about how terrible it was, think about how much it hurts, to make it better?

[raise hands]

ASK: How many of you would leave it alone to try to make it better — in other words, admit and acknowledge that it happened and that it hurt, but then let it go, to make it better?

[raise hands]

ASK: Is this different from poking at a bruise?

[brief discussion]

ASK: If you were holding a sharp rock in your hand and it kind of hurt, how many of you would squeeze it harder?

[raise hands]

ASK: How many of you would open your hand, relax your grip, or drop it?

[raise hands]

When our minds are in pain, if we are distressed, if we are unhappy, the problem is that our minds have been contaminated by memory.

Remember, we are born in a pretty much pure state, and then we have memories, and when those memories are painful, Slick sometimes plays them in our head. It gets in the way of our access to the moment. It's like static on a radio. The painful static is getting in the way of our clear signals.

When we get hurt emotionally, it makes us insecure. When we get insecure it takes us out of the clear signals of the moment because we are consumed with protecting ourselves.

This happens to everyone.

Let's say someone does a bad thing to us, and we can feel the pain. Usually without realizing it we start holding those painful thoughts in our minds, and it starts eating up our energy. Our energy is going into thinking about the past and keeps us from having a good time. If we're thinking about the past there is no room at that moment to think about the present.

ASK: After someone has done something bad to us that hurt, where is the pain coming from? Once it is over, where is the pain coming from?

[discussion]

See, it seems like the pain is coming from the person who's responsible for doing something bad to us. Most everyone thinks this way. But once they stop doing what they're doing, we are then continuing the pain ourselves by poking on the bruise. The harder we squeeze the sharp rock the more it hurts, and the more it hurts the more energy goes into it.

So we're not available for catching the pass, or having peace of mind, or being able to enjoy life. If we're dealing with the pain, we're not dealing with the rest of what is going on in life in the moment.

Elie Wiesel was a Jewish man who was thrown into two of Hitler's concentration camps during World War II. He suffered more abuses and torture than most of us could ever imagine. Years later he said, "We have a responsibility not to let them kill us a second time. The first time they are responsible. The second time, we are responsible."

ASK: What do you think he meant by this?

[discussion ~ someone may bring up that it means that we can't let other people do things like that again, and that's true, but there is also another meaning]

Those memories of what happened to us are in our heads. When it was happening it was absolutely horrible. Now that it's not happening anymore the only thing that can make us feel horrible is if we let those memories keep us in horrible feelings "a second time."

ASK: Can anyone say what the difference is between this and denying that something bad happened, or denying that you feel pain?

[discussion]

When someone is in denial, that person pretends that something bad didn't happen, or they pretend that they are not in pain. This does not work because deep down inside we know that it did happen, that we did get hurt, and no matter what we say to ourselves about it our mind knows better. We can't fool our minds. So we still end up feeling yucky — it just might be in different ways.

Instead, here, we are saying, "Yes, this thing happened, and it was painful, and now that we know it happened and we know how painful it was, it's now up to us to let it go."

Once again we are at the fork in the road. Something bad happens to us, we get hurt. Now we are at a fork in the road. This time the road has three forks.

[draw a line on the board with three prongs at the end of it]

On one path, we hold onto the pain, think about it hard, deal with how much it hurts.

ASK: What is down the road for us if we take this path? What is likely to happen?

[entertain ideas]

We may get deeper into the pain and get consumed — eaten up — by it.

On another path, we deny that anything bad happened or that we got hurt.

ASK: What's down the road on this path? What happens to us?

[entertain ideas]

When we deny that anything happened or that we were hurt, the path may be clear for a while but eventually we'll fall into a hole. It will come back on us in some way.

On the other path, we admit that something bad happened and that it hurt, but then we let it go.

ASK: What is down the road on this path?

[entertain ideas]

More peace of mind.

ASK: What happens if we put it out of our minds but then it comes back on us again? Don't answer this now. This will be answered in the next session.

So, let's get back to one secret to doing well.

When we're caught up in painful memories, we don't want them to do any more harm to us than they already have done, so we can admit that they happened, and then let them go. See them now as just thoughts from our memory that don't have to hurt us any more.

This works because of our innate health, that natural wisdom in us. Whenever a painful memory comes to mind we can be sure that our innate wisdom delivered it to us at the time it did because we were ready to see it for what it was, and move on. This is part of the natural healing process. Anything we do with the memory, other than let it come and go, would interfere with that natural process and it wouldn't help us. In fact, it may harm us because it keeps us in lowered spirits.

If a little pollution is poured into a river, left to nature it will eventually be cleansed as it goes downstream. The only thing that will stop the cleansing is if we keep pouring more pollution into the river.

We can open up our hand and let the sharp, painful rock fall to the ground. When we let the memory come and go on its own, we eventually come to peace with it.

ASK: So, let's say we are walking around with a hurt associated with a painful memory and we want to get rid of our pain, what might we want to do?

[through the discussion, when it appears to be the right time, either reveal this chart, or construct it as you go along by writing it on the board]

FOR HURT TO GO AWAY

1. Decide: I don't want to hold on to the hurt any more than is natural.

2. Admit: I am now hurting myself by continuing to hold onto my own thinking, even though what happened is over now.

3. Allow the memory to flow through. Let it go.

4. If it doesn't go away, we could even forgive.

[an explanation of each item follows]

1. Decide: I don't want to hold on to the hurt anymore.

The idea is to understand that it is not good for us to keep living with the hurt of this memory and to decide that we don't want to hold on to it anymore, or the feelings and thoughts associated with it. Bad memories will naturally surface when we are strong enough to deal with them, when we are ready to let them pass through. In other words, when we are in healthy functioning a passing thought, no matter how horrible the thought, cannot harm us.

2. Admit: I am now hurting myself with my own thinking.

The idea is to know that it happened and know that it hurt when it did, but that now it is only a thought from our memories that we are carrying into the present. The bad situation no longer exists; only our thinking does. It was horrible then, but if the situation has ended it is only a thought now. Now we are only hurting ourselves with our thoughts. This can sometimes be a tough thing to admit.

[IMPORTANT NOTE: Some students may be involved in ongoing situations that are harmful. This will be dealt with at the end of this session. If it comes up in the discussion now, they need to know that it is really important for them to let someone know (either you or a guidance counselor or someone they trust) because otherwise they are going to keep living with that pain.]

3. Allow the memory to flow through and let it go.

The appearance of the painful memory is natural. Allowing it to flow through is natural. We're the only ones that can keep it stuck. If the hurt is in the past, and we are the only ones keeping it alive now, it is in our power to let it flow on through, to drop it or dismiss it or ignore it because we know it is not serving us well — and not allow ourselves to keep hurting ourselves with it by holding onto it.

4. If you can't seem to let it go, we could even forgive.

[Note: We realize that forgiveness is extremely controversial, and some people get quite upset when they hear this. But please allow us to explain what we mean by this and why we think it is useful:]

It is natural for thoughts like this to keep coming back to us from time to time. If they are coming back so often that they are interfering with our lives and we can't seem to let them go or dismiss them, it may be a signal that we are continuing to hold on to something that we may not be aware of. Perhaps we are blaming somebody for causing us the pain, or we hate them for doing it to us. It makes sense for people who have been harmed to feel that way. Unfortunately, to keep feeling that way doesn't do us much good. We may need to change the way we see it. To truly be able to be rid of the pain, we may find that we need to forgive the person. We are not forgiving the harm they caused! We are not saying that they shouldn't have to pay for their crimes or their abuse — because they should. We are forgiving because we're the ones that are carrying around the pain, and it is only hurting us.

We are forgiving them because "they know not what they do." In other words, they had to be completely misguided to do what they did. They had to be completely lost in their messed up, crazy thinking. If they had been able to see in a different way whatever they saw that let them do this at the time, they wouldn't have done it. If they thought differently, they would have done it differently. They were innocent in the sense that they couldn't see a better way at the time. But they still have to pay! It is no excuse. Forgiveness is not something we do for them. Forgiveness is something we do for ourselves. Forgiveness is like taking an eraser and wiping the board clean so that we can finally move on. Sometimes forgiveness can be a really hard thing to do, but people have done it and they felt relieved. Oh yes, we can even forgive ourselves for not being able to let go of the pain, or not being able to forgive someone else. Even that helps.

ASK: What about if a trauma is going on right now, and it is ongoing, what should someone do?

[discussion]

Safety is always the first issue. If this is happening to you, it is absolutely critical to make a good plan to ensure your own safety, including talking to some adult you trust. Even if the person doing it has told you not to tell anyone, you've got to understand that by not telling anyone you will continue to be hurt, and you're worth more than that.

The other thing to do is to try to remember to keep a clear head. That will help you know what to do, because you will be able to rely on your wisdom to guide you. One thing that may help you to keep a clear head is to recognize that the person causing the trauma is lost and misguided. See how lost they are, how messed up and crazy their thinking is. But a clear head will protect you from being suckered in again if they apologize and say they'll never do it again. If you listen to that little cool voice of wisdom you will hear it say to you to be careful when you need to be, to only trust someone when you really can. A clear head will also help you to do whatever you need to do to protect yourself at all times.

ASK: Do you think someone can survive something really bad and still have a perfectly fine life?

[discussion]

If they do not keep thinking those painful thoughts, they will have other thoughts. Other happier, more peaceful thoughts will have room to pop in.

F. Home Practice

Practice letting thoughts flow through and letting go — of whatever it is that is not serving you well by holding onto those thoughts.

G. Summary

Ideally we would like students to be saying to themselves, "Wait a minute, you mean the pain and hurt I am feeling now is coming from my own mind squeezing that painful memory!? And to get rid of it, I just have to know that it isn't good for me, and not want to feel the hurt any more, and let it go — open the hand so the rock drops out?"

[A further note about traumas. In this session we talked about dealing with hurts, and traumas are big, huge hurts. There has been a great deal of controversy about how some therapists have treated their clients' traumas. Health Realization offers an entirely different approach. As suggested in this session, traumas from the past reveal themselves when we are ready (strong enough) to deal with them. They will pop into our heads when triggered by something, and over time a natural healing process will occur if we let those thoughts pass through, which will allow us to begin to see the trauma with more perspective. The question is, do we want to allow the trauma to shape and define the rest of our lives? We can recognize that we have it in our power to not allow the memory of a trauma to rule our lives. We are not damaged goods! We are healthy, wise people who have temporarily gotten off track because of the thinking associated with it, and thoughts can change.]

TO SOLVE A PERSONAL PROBLEM

1. ADMIT that you're not seeing something right and that you don't know what to do

2. HOPE to see it in a new way

3. Have FAITH and TRUST that you'll be able to solve it

4. CLEAR YOUR HEAD and wait for the answer to come when you're ready

Session Twenty-One

Dealing Effectively With Others

A. To Teachers

The purpose of this session is to help the students understand that they — and we — are all doing the best they know how at the time, given the way they see things. We have all done things at certain times that, had we seen it then the way we see it now, we wouldn't have acted that way. In that sense, we are all innocent. Everything we do makes sense to us at the time, though it may not make any sense to us later.

Because we are all this way to varying degrees, it is possible to see others' actions with humility and compassion and even forgiveness — because we've all been in similar places at various times, even if they are not nearly to the extreme of some of our other fellow human beings.

This holds true even for people who commit the worst crimes — even for perpetrators of sexual abuse or children who bring guns or knives to school intending to harm teachers or other students. The fact is, that is the only way they know how to be. For some reason they think they need to do what they do. They can't help it in the sense that they are stuck following their thinking. This in no way excuses their behavior; it is absolutely inexcusable, and they should be held accountable for their harmful actions. But if they saw life differently, they would act differently. And unless they come to think differently, their actions will not change.

Feeling compassion for someone has nothing to do with holding people accountable for their offenses. As suggested in the previous session it has much more to do with relieving our own burden of bad feelings. To hold grudges against them, to hate them, only hurts ourselves. They're not the ones feeling our pain. Our hate is doing nothing for them. If we do not have compassion — if for no other reason than to see or realize what they had to go through in their own lives as they were growing up to develop the thinking they did — we are the only ones keeping ourselves in a painful state. Yes, they still have to pay, but to see people in their innocence, to see them with compassion, is to relieve ourselves of the burden so we can live in nicer feelings instead of continuing to feel pain.

In smaller ways, it also holds that when we treat all others in a nice way, even if they are nasty to us, it protects us from their bad feelings, and it may even do them some good. After all, they are acting out of fear and insecurity, and if we can relieve some of that fear they may respond better.

This is also true when dealing with students. When we look out at our classrooms filled with students who behave in all kinds of ways, some not terribly kind or productive, it is helpful to keep in mind that learning happens best when insecurities subside. Therefore, it is in our own best interests as teachers to help even the most incorrigible students feel secure when they are around us. When we accomplish this, the better they will learn, and the better they will behave for us.

To create the best foundation for dealing with others, we must recognize that how we see the person will determine how we act toward them. We are all capable of seeing each person's inherent, natural health, and knowing that people really want to function in that way. Their health has only been obscured by insecure thoughts. We can then take the responsibility to move the relationship in the right direction by suspending judgments and criticism.

B. Key Points

◆ We are all doing the best we know how at the time, given the way we see things.

◆ Because we have all done things that made sense to us at the time, we can see others in their innocence (because they couldn't see what they were doing), with humility (because we've been there too, in our own way), and with compassion (because they must be hurting very much themselves to do harm to others).

Sample Questions for Reflective Discussion

Have you discovered anything that is beneficial for you in dealing with others?

What do you think this statement means: that everyone is always doing the best they know how to do at the time, given the way they see things? Do you believe that, and why?

What do you think it means that everyone is always acting out of innocence? Do you believe that, and why?

What do you think this discussion means for you when you are having trouble dealing with somebody?

C. Needed Materials

prepared chart of "To Deal With Others — " (see end of session)

D. Opening Statement

In the last session we considered how to deal with ourselves when bad stuff happens. In this session we will consider how to deal with others, especially when they are difficult, or when we believe that they are causing us harm. This can even happen sometimes with parents and teachers and principals — and even sometimes with our friends.

E. Activity/Story Line

This is a true story: Rick, a freshman in high school, had an agreement with his aunt and uncle that he could borrow their snow machine (snowmobile) whenever he wanted, provided that he stayed on their property, didn't go too fast, and didn't cross any roads. He also had per-mission to ride on the land next door where a friend of his lived. So one day Rick rode up to his friend's house and they had a good time riding around together. They then had the idea to go riding on a nice hilly field across the road. Rick thought to himself, "That'll be fun." Then he thought, "But I'm not supposed to go across the road with the machine." Then he thought, "It'll only be for a little while. It won't do any harm." Then he thought, "Do I really want to do this?" Then he thought, "They won't know." So he said, "Okay, let's go." He got to the edge of the road, looked both ways, started to head across, and got hit by a car coming around the curve. One ski of the snow machine broke the car window as Rick went flying across the road and landed in (luckily) a soft snow bank. The snow machine was wrecked, and he could easily have been killed. His aunt and uncle were grateful that he was alive, but Rick had betrayed their trust and left them without an expensive piece of machinery they used around the farm.

ASK: What do you think was the seemingly unimportant decision that Rick made at the time that got him into so much trouble and, in fact, nearly killed him?

[brief discussion]

Sometimes we get thoughts that appear not to be very important at the time, but if we follow them, they could lead to disasters later on.

ASK: Suppose someone is being verbally abusive to you, or hurts you, or bugs you in some way. What do you think is going on inside that person?

[brief discussion]

As we saw in previous sessions, the reason they act that way is that they've gotten insecure, and they just don't know what else to do. Probably without their knowing it, their pain or fear or insecurity is driving them to do something to make them feel better. It is just coming out all wrong.

ASK: Let's say we hate this person, or are mad or feel badly toward him or her in some other way. Which one of us suffers, that person or us? Why?

[discussion]

We're the ones who suffer. They don't even know we're having nasty thoughts about them unless someone tells them. We are the ones left with the bad feelings. We are the ones who end up feeling distress, or unhappiness, or anger, or dissatisfaction, or worry. That feeling carried in us hurts us. Is that the way we want to live?

Here's a story that will help us see what's going on:

STORY: Dr. Jeckyll was a kind, compassionate doctor and chemist, living in Europe in the mid 1800s. He was experimenting with chemicals that would alter the brain and body to enhance its healing process. The experiment went terribly wrong, and it took over his body. It turned him into a mean, nasty creature named Mr. Hyde, who terrorized people in the community. But he would only do that when the chemicals were active. When they wore off he would go back to being his kind, gentle, compassionate self. Yet he kept going back and forth, and he didn't have control over it.

In a way, we are all Dr. Jeckylls and Mr. Hydes. We have both of those parts in us to varying degrees.

When we're in low moods we turn into Mr. Hyde. When we're in good moods we're like Dr. Jeckyll.

Behind every troubling person is a healthy Dr. Jeckyll wanting to come out.

When we look at someone who appears to be a mean, nasty person, it's just that their Mr. Hyde is more out there, more on the surface. But the Dr. Jeckyll is still in there, waiting to come out.

What if we could see the Dr. Jeckyll in everyone? If she or he is in us, even when we're in a terrible mood, she or he is in everyone. If we saw the Dr. Jeckyll within that person we would automatically feel warmer to him or her.

If we see the Mr. Hyde side, suppose we saw it as just a trait that happens when s/he gets insecure — as the armor the person uses when s/he gets afraid. What if we knew that when that person gets secure again s/he steps out of the armor and becomes a more likable person.

That person may never show the Dr. Jeckyll side to us — but only because s/he's too insecure around us to show it.

So it is possible to feel kindly even toward someone who appears to be the worst person. All we have to do is see beyond those behaviors to the good will behind the person. How does the worst person have any good will? Because that person wants to live in nice feelings just like we do. S/he just doesn't have a clue how to go about it. That person — every person — is only doing their best they know how to do, given the way they see it at the time.

All people, deep down, feel like they mean well. They just don't know a better way. Their thinking is so far off that their behaviors are far off. Everyone wants to be a good person. We just don't always know how.

ASK: If we see the person that way, there is a reward waiting. Does anyone know what that reward might be?

[brief discussion]

It feels good to feel kindly even toward someone whose Mr. Hyde is showing — even if someone is mean to us — if we know s/he is just insecure. If we see the insecurity behind the behavior we will see the person differently and we will feel differently toward them, and that will probably make us act differently when we're around them.

A bully at a school thought he controlled all the students in his class. He would call them nasty names. He would beat them up. He would make them give him their money. Everyone was afraid of him. One day his teacher walked into the school lavatory and found that his classmates had written foul things about the bully on the wall. She brought him into the bathroom to show him and said, "See, you think you control the other kids but look at what they think of you. If you were nicer to them they would think differently about you." The bully bullied his classmates because he thought it was making them respect him. But it was having the opposite effect. He wanted to be respected. He never got that at home. He just got bullied at home by his parents and older brothers. That was all he knew how to do because it was all that he saw and all that he experienced. So he began to treat the other kids in a nicer way. At first they were shocked and didn't trust it, but soon they warmed up to him and he began to make friends. That was all he really wanted. He just didn't know how to go about it because his thinking was messed up.

ASK: Which do you think feels better — to feel kind feelings, or to feel nasty, hateful, or miserable feelings?

[brief discussion]

In other words, it's better for us to feel kindly toward someone than angry, hostile, nasty, or miserable. The reward for us is that *we* feel better.

And, here's the kicker: it also may help the other person.

ASK: How do you think it would help the other person?

[brief discussion]

If we see the good in them, if we have faith in them, if they feel it from us, it has more of a tendency to pull out the Dr. Jeckyll in them. It's harder for Mr. Hyde to function under those circumstances. It brings the Mr. Hydes to their senses and they respond better.

See, we've got to remember that we're all like this. We all sometimes have our Mr. Hydes showing, and sometimes our Dr. Jeckylls. If we are like that, and we see someone else being that way, we could see them with compassion, because they must be really hurting to be that way, and we could feel a little humility because we've been there too in our own way — only not as extreme. We haven't always been so kind to all others.

Compassion is identifying with how we're all the same way. It makes us feel humble to know that we bug others or harm others sometimes when we don't want to.

When we see people in this way, it is like reaching out a hand to them and stretching so they can grab it and help pull them out of what they're stuck in. They will probably resist at first. But it is awfully hard to resist kind feelings when they keep coming and coming.

Sometimes they won't take the good will at all, but that's up to them. If they want to keep feeling miserable that's their own business.

And all we have to do is see behind the insecurity to the loving person inside, to the Dr. Jeckyll inside, to the good will inside, and overlook the Mr. Hyde parts. That Dr. Jeckyll is there in each and every person. And the person may even act better around us that way.

ASK: Won't seeing people this way make them walk all over us? How many of you think this?

[brief discussion]

When we look closely at it, we will see that this really has nothing to do with it. We're talking about how we feel inside toward the other person, that's all. All we're saying is, this is how to see people's crazy personalities and bad habits. It is protection for us. Our wisdom and common sense is more available to us when we see people this way.

Compassion protects us from our own bad feelings. It keeps us on an even keel. And when that happens our minds are more calm and, as we learned in other sessions, that is when our healthy, inner self kicks in and gives us a solid foundation to operate from.

It's better for ourselves to be in touch with our wisdom instead of running scared around the person. In this way, we can see how to deal with the other person in a way that protects us. The other way, we're just scrambling and mixed up, and we could get more hurt.

ASK: Let's say that someone yells at you. What do you think will happen if you yell back? Do you think they will get more upset or less upset?

[briefly entertain ideas]

ASK: What happens if they get more upset?

[briefly entertain ideas]

If they get more insecure, it makes them more upset or angry, and it makes things worse.

ASK: Let's take the person who yells at you. Suppose, instead of yelling back, you understand that the person is upset, that their Mr. Hyde is out there, and if they were their Dr. Jeckyll self they wouldn't be acting this way, and they really don't mean it — that person is just temporarily acting like a lunatic, and you'd better keep your distance and wait for the opportunity when s/he's calmed down to respond. What do you think would happen then?

[brief discussion]

S/he would be more likely to calm down and respond better.

It's like being in a hurricane. It's blowing and roaring furiously. But in the middle, there's a peaceful, calm eye.

[illustration of a hurricane with an eye in the middle — or draw it on the board]

Understanding and compassion keep people in the calm eye of the hurricane. Feeling insecurity, anger, judgment, upset, bothered, keeps you in the hurricane.

Here is another way to look at this:

ASK: Do you think you could get any points against Michael Jordan if you were playing basketball against him one-on-one?

Suppose you were on a very shiny, slippery basketball court, and Michael Jordan could only wear a pair of very slippery socks, and you were wearing a pair of the best gripping rubber-soled sneakers that you've ever seen. Do you think you could get any points off him then?

You may not win, but it would certainly even up the game a little.

When you feel compassion and understanding for someone it's like playing in the best rubber-soled sneakers. It's our choice which shoes we put on our feet to play this game.

If someone is giving us a hard time and we lose our bearings and take things personally, or blame, or judge, or get angry, or get scared, or get annoyed or upset, we get distracted and we can't see what people are up to. But by having an understanding feeling toward the other person, we're clearing our heads and it will be more likely that the person will find their bearings. That's what gives us the traction, like the sneakers.

Will that be enough? Maybe, maybe not.

But if the problem is that people are feeling insecure and in low moods, wouldn't the solution be the opposite?

ASK: What is the opposite of insecurity?

[entertain ideas]

Security, well-being, love, understanding, compassion.

That's what we want to give to other people, so they will act less badly to us. This is why it's good for us — for our own benefit alone — to act this way. The most selfish thing for us to do in dealing with difficult people — to get the best results for ourselves — is to feel kindly toward them. That's what will both protect us most and make us feel best.

Strange, isn't it?

Besides, our acting that way is like holding a mirror up to the other person's face: Suppose someone is yelling and screaming at us, and we're really nice to them, wouldn't that put a lot of pressure on them? Think of it for yourself: Suppose you yell and scream at someone, and s/he doesn't yell back and is just nice in return. Wouldn't you start to wonder what you were doing?

In an atmosphere of understanding, people are puzzled by their own behavior. If you yell back, it shows the other person that they must be right — because they're getting to you. What they're doing gets reinforced.

And even if they never change when you're nice to them, if you're with them for two hours, at least you've spent two hours feeling nicer instead of two hours feeling miserable.

ASK: From all the things you have heard so far in these sessions, what are some ways that you think would help you deal with people who are difficult for you or who give you a hard time or that do harm to you?

[list on the board]

[discussion. Prepare a chart of key points to reveal at the end of the discussion, as follows]

To help us deal with others, we can —

◆ see with understanding; see their insecurity

◆ see their innocence

◆ have compassion

◆ have humility

- see the big picture: take it less personally

- see with humor

- even forgive

[point to chart —]

Here is a way to sum up what we can do to help us deal with people:

- Understand that when people harm or bother others, they are acting out of insecurity.

We are all part Dr. Jeckyll and part Mr. Hyde. Mr. Hyde is driven by insecurity. Just like Slick. Jeckyll is covered up by Slick Hyde at those times. At those times, the person really didn't understand what they were doing. And if they did know exactly what they were doing, it's that they didn't know a better way at the time.

- See people as basically innocent.

Because we are all like Mr. Hyde sometimes, we all do things sometimes that we wouldn't have done if we had our wits about us. Again, we couldn't do any better at the time because we couldn't see anything else at that time. In that sense we are innocent. Looking back on it we wish we hadn't done those things. That's because we see it differently now. But then, we acted because of the way we saw it. We couldn't have done any better at the time, given the way we saw it. We are always innocently doing our best at the time in this way.

Does being innocent mean that we don't have to pay for the wrongs we do? No! No! Absolutely not. We have to pay. Others have to pay. But given the way we saw it at that time that is all we knew how to do.

And that goes for everyone else who is doing bad things to us.

- See people with compassion

Can you imagine the pain and insecurity that person must have to live with to treat me that way?

- See people with humility

Gee, we do bad things to others sometimes without knowing what we're doing. We're like them at those times, and we don't realize it when we're doing it either.

- See it less personally

When we're old and looking back on our lives, a lot of the things that bother us now won't bother us any more. If we are capable of seeing it differently then, we're capable of seeing it differently now. It's all a matter of thought, and it's all part of life.

◆ See it with humor

See life as a comedy of errors. We're all in a big play — a TV situation comedy — and we do the strangest things to each other, most of which we have no idea about because most of our thinking is hidden from us in the same way that we can't see most of an iceberg.

◆ See the person with forgiveness

As we've noted, people can be forgiven "because they know not what they do." Remember, forgiving is like taking a messy blackboard and going over it with a wet eraser. Forgiving cleanses us of being affected badly by the person trying to do us harm. *[Note: You can demonstrate this by erasing the board to make the point.]*

ASK: Can anyone think of any problems that might come up that may make seeing others in any of these ways a bad idea?

[discussion]

Some people think that if you see people as innocent or with compassion or forgive them, it says that what they did was okay. Not so! What they did was not okay. All those deeper feelings do is keep our own mind uncontaminated so we're not running scared.

Some people think that to change the wrongs of the world and fight injustice, we need to be angry to do it. But that's not true. There is no link. People can do things like try to save the environment just because they think it's the right thing to do.

Holding grudges is unproductive. Seeing with these deep feelings is the most helpful thing we can do for ourselves because it leaves our minds free from the burden of grudges. It is a great burden for ourselves to live in angry or hurtful feelings. These feelings for others clear the passageway of our minds, which in turn, brings us more mental health.

F. Home Practice

Bring someone to mind that you have difficulty with. How might you deal with them in a way that makes it less likely that you will be upset by them or bothered by them, or hurt by them?

G. Summary/Conclusion

Ideally, students would be saying to themselves, "If someone is giving me a hard time and I get upset or angry or scared or annoyed or judge them, I will be distracted and won't be able to see what people are up to. But by having an understanding of the other person and seeing them in a better way, I'll be helping myself and possibly even be helping them out at the same time."

TO HELP US DEAL WITH OTHERS

- see with understanding; see their insecurity

- see their innocence

- have compassion

- have humility

- see the big picture: take it less personally

- see with humor

- have forgiveness

Session Twenty-Two

Seemingly Unimportant Decisions: Justifying Behavior

A. To Teachers

If we take a look at people who are the most disruptive, most destructive, most withdrawn, most problematic, they all share a common phenomenon. They all make decisions that justify their behavior to themselves.

On the surface, such decisions seem unimportant. Yet, these are the very decisions that fuel their destructive cycle of behavior. When people make excuses to themselves about their behaviors, a road opens before them where nearly any extreme behavior becomes possible.

In this session we will go to the extreme so students will be able to see some of most destructive problem cycles at work in problem individuals. We will use the example of sexual abuse. The purpose of going this route is to show how the mind works in creating behaviors where they could not in a million years imagine how anyone could do such things. If young people can see the mechanism in the extreme, the hope is that they will see how the same mechanism is at work in all of us in even minor ways that get us into difficulties, where decisions that seem unimportant at the time but are actually steppingstones down a road of trouble.

Unfortunately a few students out there may be able to relate all too well to this example. Such students have serious thinking problems, and the hope is that this will serve as a wake up call for them, to head them off from proceeding further down that path. But don't assume that any student who identifies with this process has either experienced or perpetrated sexual abuse.

[Note: In this session it will be important for the teacher to watch the students carefully and if anyone is having a particularly hard time be sure some appropriate supports are available for them.]

B. Key Points

◆ If we look closely, we make decisions every day that don't seem to be important at the time, or that we tell ourselves aren't important, that start a cycle down a particular fork in the road, or continue a behavior by convincing us that what we are doing is okay.

◆ The more we are aware of how we think ourselves into justifying these seemingly unimportant decisions, the less control they have over us.

Sample Questions for Reflective Discussion

When you are about to make a choice about something that you know is not a good thing to do, and you've little voices in your head, some telling you to do it, some telling you not to do it, others telling you that if you just do this one little part that it'll be okay, how do you know which voice to listen to?

If at each decision point we are at a fork in the road, which voices will lead you down which path?

C. Needed Materials

None

D. Opening Statement

ASK: Were you able to see a difficult person (for you) in a different way? Did it make you feel any differently? Did it make you do anything differently?

[discussion]

In this session we're going to look at some decisions we make. We'll start with an old joke.

You're in an airplane. The airplane pilot comes over the intercom to speak to the passengers, and says, "I've got good news, and bad news."

"The good news is, we've got tail winds. We're making very good time."

"The bad news is, we're lost!"

ASK: What do you think the significance of that old joke is for people's lives?

[discussion]

Sometimes it looks as though we're doing well, proceeding well along our path, but we've lost sight of something very important. And if we don't slow down to take a look, we may be racing down a path that can lead to problems or, worse, destruction.

Every day the newspaper is filled with stories about people who commit acts that are so bad that we wonder, "How could anyone do anything like that!?" Those people are racing out of control down problem paths, often without knowing what they are doing or where they are going. And even if they do know what they are doing, they are faced with decisions at every step along the way that could turn them around. Yet, in their thinking, they somehow manage to justify those decisions to themselves. The decisions seem unimportant at the time, but each one is another step in the direction of problems and away from health. This may not make too much sense right now, but maybe this story will help.

[NOTE: IMPORTANT REMINDER!!! A story is offered in this session about the development of a sexually abused sexual perpetrator that may strike a chord in some kids who have been in or are in similar situations either as victims or as perpetrators. It is very important before running this session to have a support system in place to help students who might need it!]

E. Activity/Story Line

Here is an example. We say to ourselves, "How could any adult, or anyone, commit sexual abuse on a child? That's so disgusting!"

ASK: Why don't the perpetrators think it's disgusting like you do?

[discussion]

People think differently because of their different thoughts and beliefs they carry around, but some sexual perpetrators do think it's disgusting, they hate themselves for doing it, and they still do it.

ASK: How do you think that could happen?

[brief discussion]

Their feelings are compelling them to do stuff that even they might not think is right, but at every step along the way they are at a decision point — another fork in the road — where they justify to themselves that what they're doing is okay. Each of those decision points seems like it's not very important at the time, but each one of those decisions is another step along the wrong path. The further along the path they go the deeper into it they get and the harder it is to go back.

Let's take a look at what some of the "seemingly unimportant decisions" and justifications that sexual abusers might use.

Suppose a man gets a feeling. He loves little kids. But his love is perverted because he gets sexual feelings about them. First, we might think, "Yuck! How could anyone have that feeling!?"

ASK: Does anyone have any ideas about where anyone could get a feeling like that?

[briefly entertain ideas]

ASK: Well, it does come from their thoughts, but where do you think thoughts like that could have come from?

[discussion]

[Note to teacher: change name if you have a Jason in class] Here is a story: Jason grew up in a home where his father left before he was two years old. His mother Marie didn't know much about being a parent and didn't know how to handle him. She wasn't very warm to him, and she yelled at him all the time. When Jason was four years old his mother brought home a new boyfriend, he got her pregnant, and they were married in four months.

At first Jason's stepfather Andrew was very nice to him. He always brought Jason candy and stuff and took him places, and Jason liked him. Andrew would always put his arm around him and hug him, and that made Jason feel nice. One day when Jason was six his stepfather was tickling him, and Andrew touched Jason in a place where Jason didn't think he should be touched. But maybe it was just an accident.

The next time it happened Jason knew it was no accident, and he tried to run away, but Andrew grabbed him and told him not to be afraid, that he loved him, and just wanted to show him how much he loved him, and that he shouldn't tell anyone — especially his mother, because she wouldn't understand and would send him away if she found out.

Jason began to hate those times with his stepfather. But it was tender and loving and did feel good physically (in spite of himself), plus Andrew kept giving him presents as long as he kept doing it and kept quiet.

ASK: What do you think Jason's thinking might have been coming out of a situation like that?

[discussion]

What happened in this case was that by the time Jason was sixteen, in his mind, without really being aware of it, he believed that sex with children was how one showed and received love. He didn't like the thought of it, but he didn't even know that it had gotten into his mind like that. He tried going out with a girl, but things didn't work right and it ended up being a terrible experience.

One day he saw a six-year-old kid that he found himself really attracted to. It surprised him. The thought of it repulsed him. But in his private thoughts he started to wonder what it would be like.

ASK: What do you think is going on in Jason's mind now?

[briefly entertain ideas]

ASK: What decision point is Jason at?

[discussion]

In Jason's mind, the decision was not very important. It was, "I wonder if I should be thinking about him like this?" His answer was, "Well, thinking about him doesn't do anybody any harm."

ASK: What do you think his answer did to him?

[entertain ideas]

That thought justified his decision. The decision was seemingly unimportant; his response justified it, and so he started down a path.

ASK: What are some other answers to Jason's question that he may have come up with?

[brief discussion]

Next, Jason found himself having fantasies about what it would be like to be with this kid. He was at another decision point.

ASK: What decision point was he at?

[brief discussion]

Suppose when he had this fantasy he got really turned on. He was sexually aroused and wanted to do something about it. He thought, "Should I do this?" If he concluded, "Well, it's not doing anybody harm," he would again be convincing himself that the decision was not so important, and it was another justification that sent him further down the path.

ASK: Could he turn back at this point? What would he have to do to turn back?

[briefly entertain ideas]

He could have made another decision. He could have known that it was just a thought that he should dismiss as crazy. If he was troubled by the thought and couldn't get it out of his mind, he could go to someone and seek help.

ASK: Why might Jason not have dismissed the thought?

[entertain ideas]

He probably didn't know about his thinking the way you do now, so he was stuck with it.

[brief discussion]

ASK: Why wouldn't he go to someone for help?

[entertain ideas]

Probably because, besides those thoughts, he had other thoughts that he was embarrassed about. He didn't like what he was doing and he knew that nobody else would like his secret thinking and behavior either. He didn't trust that anyone would help him. Also, his thinking may not have shown him that these behaviors were a problem he should do something about, they were just uneasy feelings at this point, and he probably didn't know like you do now that those uneasy feelings were signals that he was getting off course from his health.

Let's go on with the story. As things progressed, Jason found that there were lots of other decisions to be made. Each one was a little more complicated. Each one took a little more justification. But in his mind, if he considered the decisions to be unimportant, he may have come up with "good reasons" to justify those behaviors that would allow him to proceed farther on.

Here are some other "seemingly unimportant decisions" that Jason faced along the way:

◆ Should he go and watch the child near the playground?

◆ Should he go up and talk to him?

◆ Should he try to get him alone?

◆ Should he use drugs or alcohol to make himself feel more comfortable?

◆ Should he drive around looking for other kids?

The answers that Jason gives to each of these questions will ultimately determine whether he will end up sexually abusing this kid, or another, or getting help to move back toward health.

Along the way, especially at the beginning, the decisions do not seem so important, but each one puts him a little closer to the abuse. The next decision is only a little step further than the last one, so it doesn't seem like such a big deal. But each is filled with some anxiety, even while justifying that it won't do that much harm. What do we mean by justifications? Things like saying to himself, "Oh, that's not so bad," "I'm not really harming anyone." "The kid will end up liking it." Each similar thought that he takes seriously moves him a little closer to the abuse, so when he finally gets there it is not a huge leap, it is only one little step more.

ASK: What are some other decisions that could be made at those points, given these questions?

[entertain ideas]

ASK: If he followed your suggested decisions instead of his own justification decisions, what do you think would have happened instead?

[discussion]

So this is the process that people go through in their minds without realizing it. They don't realize they're going farther down the road with each new thought that they take seriously and don't dismiss as "just another one of those crazy thoughts" that shouldn't be followed. But it doesn't only happen with horrible things like sexual abuse, it happens with other bad things like physical abuse, it happens with alcohol and drug abuse, it happens in teenage pregnancy, and it also happens in little ways with many, many little things that happen in our own lives. So we're going to see how it might happen with, say, an issue such as smoking.

TASK: [Count off by fives so you have groups of five]. In your groups of five people, you're going to take the issue of smoking. First, make a list of all the decision points along the way. Second, go back over your list and decide what some possibilities are for each decision point, and third, explore the direction that each of those seemingly unimportant decisions could take you.

[Give each small group about 15 minutes for this activity. Each group reports back to the full group. For reporting back it is suggested that each group offer only one decision point, then ask if any other group had this one too, and ask all groups to come up with what they thought the possibilities are for each and where each might lead. Then go on to the next group with another decision point and follow the same procedure until they are all covered or you run out of time.]

ASK: How can you tell which decision to make? What can you use as your guide?

[brief discussion]

Remember, your wisdom and common sense speak to you with a different kind of voice. Can you be quiet enough or clear enough to hear it when you're thinking about whether to smoke, or will you continue to take that thinking seriously that justifies the behavior to you?

ASK: Where might you be able to go to get help if you need it?

[list possibilities]

F. Home Practice

Take an issue that you are faced with making decisions about. See if you can list all the possible decision points. Consider each a possible fork in the road. What is likely to happen at each of your decision points? Do this for something that's really important to you. We won't collect them. We won't have anyone talk about them. It's something only for you, to be helpful for only you. But if you don't want to do this assignment for any reason, you'll be having some feeling that's a signal to you. Then you're at one of those decision points. You may find yourself starting to think thoughts that justify not doing it. Which thinking are you going to follow? And, if you need help, it is better to follow the thinking that leads you to ask for it.

G. Summary/Conclusions

Ideally, the students will be saying to themselves, "Hmmm, so these little decisions I have to make along the way might move me closer to problems. If I quiet my mind and pay attention to my wisdom and common sense the conclusions I come to will lead me more away from problems and toward feeling better. Plus, if I need help I can ask for it."

The bad news is, we could be kidding ourselves about the seemingly unimportant decisions we make; the good news is, we don't have to be ruled by trying to justify those decisions.

Session Twenty-Three

Relationships And Conflict

A. To Teachers

The key to relationships is building rapport, having mutual respect, and dealing with people from a positive state of mind.

First, we're in a relationship with ourselves. If we're stuck in a traffic jam and we've got to be somewhere at a certain time and it's getting late, will it serve us well to get all riled up and bent out of shape about it? Will it make it better? Will it get us there any faster? Which person inside us would we rather live with at that time?

Next, most of us are in a relationship with a partner, and many of us with our own kids. Just like we can react to traffic, we can react to something our partner does or that our kids do. Or, we can recognize that our thoughts lead us to react to our partner or kids in a certain way that can either begin a vicious unhealthy cycle or begin a healthy constructive cycle.

In a low state it is wise to hold our tongues and wait for our moods to rise before dealing with an issue. Mostly we need to simply enjoy one another.

When we let our emotions run the show, we are allowing insecurity to run the show. Acting from a feeling of insecurity will breed acting out of insecurity.

In relationships where we are helping others, such as in a teacher-student relationship, it works best if they like being in our presence and if we can help them feel a sense of hope.

If we disagree with someone or we can't fathom what they do, we can recognize that we are each coming from our separate realities, and each side contains a grain of truth that makes each of our points real to us. Instead of sticking hard and fast to our position, instead of arguing with them, we could try to see the grain of truth in what the other person is saying. If someone in a relationship is giving us a hard time, we need to recognize that their thoughts are tricking them and they don't know any better. They think they have to act that way.

We could try to see that person with love and understanding, with warmth and compassion. We can always look beyond the old thoughts to the possibility of a fresh start. We can always see our partner or kids or students or coworkers caught up in their moods (and we in ours) and not take what they do so seriously or personally.

B. Key Points

◆ The key to relationships is building rapport, having mutual respect, and dealing with people from a positive state of mind (as opposed to a low mood or when we're riled up).

◆ Our thoughts can lead us to react to others in certain ways that can begin either a downward spiral or an upward spiral. We choose!

◆ The more we can simply enjoy one another, the better our relationships will be. When someone is doing something that bugs us, the more we can watch them with interest instead of reacting to them, the better our relationships will be.

◆ If we disagree with someone, when we try to see the grain of truth in the other side, we both usually come away with a better feeling.

◆ If someone in a relationship is giving us a hard time or hurting us, the more we step back and recognize that it's not our fault, that their thoughts are tricking them and they don't know any better so they think they have to act that way, the more we see them with understanding, warmth and compassion, the less we will be emotionally harmed.

Sample Questions for Reflective Discussion

What mistakes have you noticed that people make in relationships? What would they have to know to be able to relate to each other in a healthy way?

What do you think is the most important ingredient in a good relationship, and why?

When we're going down a problem path in a relationship, how do we know it, and what might we look at as a way to get back on track?

If we're in a low mood or are emotionally reacting to something someone says in a relationship, what do we want to do at that time for the sake of the relationship?

If someone is giving us a hard time in any kind of relationship, what do you think it would be helpful to know to protect our own frame of mind?

C. Needed Materials

Large drawing paper, crayons or pastels or markers

D. Opening Statement

ASK: Does anyone have anything to share from the home practice — not about your specific situation, but just something that you learned from this process, from what we go through, in general? What did you discover about decision points and the forks in the road?

[Note: They may not be willing to share anything. That's okay. If so, simply move on.]

Today we will apply what we've been learning to relationships.

Have you ever thought that there might be something common to good relationships and to bad ones?

There is!

E. Activity/Story Line

ASK: What do you think happens between the two people in a bad relationship?

[Note to teacher: The students may say that the two people argue or fight, but dig deeper. Ask them what they think goes on in the people's minds for them to argue or fight.]

[discussion]

Within a bad relationship, no matter who the two individual people are, ego and pride get in the way. One or both people take each other's words and behaviors personally.

ASK: What do you think happens between the two people in good relationships?

[discussion]

In good relationships, one or both avoid reacting personally to the other because they understand the true motivating factor behind negative behavior: a person's own way of seeing it that happens to differ from theirs.

ASK: What do you think is often the motivating factor behind arguing or fighting in a relationship? What fuels the fire?

[entertain ideas]

Bad moods! In low moods, friends or partners criticize each other. They see problems where none really exist.

ASK: What should a person do in a relationship if their partner comes at them in a low mood, all critical and angry and defensive?

[entertain ideas]

First, don't take the low mood personally. Know it's only their low mood talking, and don't let it get to you. If it gets bad enough, excuse yourself until he or she calms down. Try to let any upset or nasty thoughts about the other person flow out of your mind. The person wouldn't be thinking those thoughts in a good mood or talking to you like that or fighting with you in a better mood. Continuing to grind away with our thinking about the incident only keeps it alive for us.

Peoples' low mood thoughts create illusions for them. For example, in a low mood it looks like there is something really wrong with the entire relationship. But it is a wonderful thing to know that we don't have to take an illusion to heart. If there really is something wrong with the relationship we'll see it that way when we're in a higher mood too, because our wisdom and common sense will be talking to us.

Unfortunately, in a relationship people get caught up in the tense, unhappy, bad mood moments, when all they have to do is wait until the mood lifts and then have a talk in an atmosphere of good will.

ASK: What do you think "good will" means?

[brief discussion]

When people mean well, and want things to work out well.

People will always have differences because they see the world differently through their thinking, but resolution to an argument or a fight is found in an atmosphere of goodwill. If there is disagreement people can come to a reasonable meeting of the minds — if that is the intention.

TASK: *[Hand out big pieces of drawing paper and crayons or markers.]* Pair up with someone. Take the drawing paper and without preplanning or speaking to each other about what you are going to draw, sit on opposite ends of the paper and begin to draw. Draw anything you want — together! Don't stop until the paper is filled or until you both feel that it's finished.

[Give students about 5 or 10 minutes, depending on how into it they are.]

ASK: Did you get a feeling of cooperation from your partner?

[brief discussion]

ASK: Did you get a feeling of goodwill or ill-will?

[brief discussion]

ASK: Was one person dominating and the other submissive?

[brief discussion]

ASK: Did your partner infringe on your space or share it with consideration?

[brief discussion]

ASK: What thoughts did you have when you started the drawing, and as it was going on?

[discussion]

ASK: What was your mood when you started the drawing, and did it change while you were doing it?

[discussion]

ASK: If you had been in a very low mood during the drawing, what do you think would have happened?

[discussion]

ASK: What do you think is a recipe for a great relationship?

[discussion]

[In the midst of the discussion the teacher can offer the following as a suggestion. The students can add to it if they want.]

Recipe for a great relationship:

5 cups of good will

2 ½ cups of good mood

8 tablespoons of lightheartedness

3 tablespoons of fun

2 tablespoons of creativity

3 cups of letting go (of your beliefs)

100 gallons of love and understanding

not even a teaspoon of taking things personally.

One more important point about this. There are times, even in a good relationship but particularly in an uncomfortable one, where people have disagreements and conflicts.

ASK: Given what you know, if two or more people have a conflict, what is the best thing they could do to resolve it?

[entertain ideas]

They could realize that, because each of us is seeing our own realities and each person's reality makes perfect sense to each of us, we could go out of our way to discover what that grain of truth is that makes it make perfect sense to the other person. To do this, we could set aside our own position for a while and listen deeply with a quiet mind to the other person, and ask them questions like a detective (a nice one) to see if we can discover that person's grain of truth.

Once we see the grain of truth in the other's side, we will feel it and tell the other person what we realized about what they were saying from their point of view, then see if the other person is willing to get quiet enough to listen to see if s/he can see our grain of truth.

Once we see each truth clearly, we understand much more of that other person's world, and then the conflict takes on far less importance because we each feel closer to the other person's side. From there, it is much less of a leap to come together on a mutual decision, because then the task becomes to find a meeting of the minds.

Here is a story about "grains of truth." Jaime's mother wanted her to watch a child "for ten minutes" while she had an important discussion with that child's mother. Jaime agreed. Jaime then received a phone call from a friend inviting her out to dinner. After ten minutes had passed, Jaime went to her mother to tell her she had to leave to go to dinner with a friend. Her mother said, "Okay, but I'm not finished yet. I'll need another five minutes."

When five minutes had passed, Jaime came down ready to leave. Her mother said, "I'll need another minute. Then I'll drive you over there." Frustrated, Jaime said, "Well, can I walk then?" Her mom said, "You can walk if you want to, but I'll need another minute."

Jaime left. When her mother finished the conversation she discovered that the child had been left alone.

Later, when Jaime returned, her mother yelled at Jaime for leaving the child alone. She said, "You told me you would watch this child while I talked to her mother. That was totally irresponsible!"

Jaime said, "I did. You said it would take ten minutes, and I did it for even more than that. You said I could walk, so I did. I didn't know it was so important about this kid."

Her mother said, "That's not true, Jaime, I told you."

Instead of a meeting of the minds, they had a butting of the heads.

ASK: Can you see the grain of truth in both their sides? What are they?

[entertain ideas]

The mother's truth: Left alone, the child could have gotten hurt, and it was dangerous to have walked out on her.

Jaime's truth: When her mother said she could walk, she thought she had permission to leave.

When they were able to step back and see each other's truth from their views, they were each able to see that the other person meant no harm. In fact, what each of them did made perfect sense — from each of their perspectives. Each was acting out of what they thought was right. When they realized this, they both naturally apologized and both of them knew what they needed to do to be more clear next time. A meeting of the minds had occurred naturally.

Until that meeting of the minds there was only conflict.

[Note to teacher: In some schools, students have been taught courses in "conflict resolution." Traditionally, these courses teach people to use "I messages" and to seek negotiation and compromise. Health Realization presents a different and, we think, a more productive approach. The problem with "I messages" (even though they are far better than "you messages") is that they focus the people on themselves and their own positions. They then try to negotiate a compromise from those positions. Through Health Realization, people are asked to take a step back from their "I" positions and listen deeply from a quiet mind for the grain of truth in the other's side. Once they each sincerely try to see it and do — if they don't, they ask the person to say it again in a different way or to tell them more — they don't have to compromise because they naturally want to go out of their way to come to a meeting of the minds. If your students have been exposed to traditional conflict resolution, you may have to point out the differences.]

TASK: Pair up with someone you haven't paired up with yet in these sessions. Bring to mind a conflict you've recently had with someone. Explain to your partner what the conflict was about. Then state both positions of the conflict. Then see if you can find the grain of truth in what the other person was saying. Your partner here might be able to help you see the other person's grain of truth because s/he has a certain distance from it that you may not have.

[give them 10 minutes for this activity, so both people in a group have a chance to do it.]

ASK: Were you able to see the other person's grain of truth? Why couldn't you see it before? And what would have happened if you were able to see it during the conflict?

[discussion]

ASK: What did you learn today about relationships and about dealing with conflict in them?

[discussion]

F. Home Practice

The next time you find yourself reacting to a friend or a family member, or a classmate, make note of it. See what their mood was. See what yours was. See whether you took it personally. See whether you can drop the matter or your feelings of being upset. See whether you can find the grain of truth in the other person's side. See whether you can come to a meeting of the minds. Were you satisfied with the way it came out?

G. Summary

Ideally, the students will be saying something like, "In a relationship, I really need to put out good will and understanding. In a conflict, if I can quiet my mind enough to listen to the other person's view instead of to my own thinking, we will have a better chance of resolving it because it will be easier to come to a meeting of the minds. And even if it doesn't, we tried."

Recipe for a Great Relationship

5 cups of good will

2½ cups of good mood

8 tablespoons of lightheartedness

3 tablespoons of fun

2 tablespoons of creativity

3 cups of letting go (of your beliefs)

100 gallons of love and understanding

not a teaspoon of taking things personally

Session Twenty-Four

Peer Pressure

A. To Teachers

Peer pressure is only a problem for people who think that what their peers think is important.

Some people do not have many thoughts about what their peers think. Some of these people may be oblivious — they simply go through their lives without noticing what other people think of them. Others don't care what others think. Still others realize their peers have thoughts about them but it doesn't bother them because they understand that those thoughts are a product of their peers' insecurity. Whatever their reasons, none of these people feel peer pressure. This means that it is possible for people — even for kids in school — not to feel peer pressure, or at least not feel it as much.

We have the free will to think whatever thoughts we want — and we do! We can think in healthy or unhealthy ways. We can think in healthy ways about peer pressure.

If we take a step back from it, we would notice that we are not affected by everything that our peers think. We are only affected by some of those things. What makes the difference? If we are already sensitive about a particular issue — for example if we care whether the way we dress looks cool or fashionable or, conversely, if we're embarrassed that our family is too poor to buy good clothes — we will react to anything our peers say about the way we dress. The issue of concern over the image we project in our clothes was already there for us in our own thinking. Therefore, that is what we would feel peer pressure about. We only feel pressured about what already concerns us. Since young people are so concerned about looking cool or being accepted in such a variety of ways, they are more subject to intense peer pressure. Yet, if they can see the pressure comes from their own thinking instead of "their peers out there," they will begin to feel less pressure.

B. Key Points

◆ We have free will to think whatever we want; meaning, we can take to heart what our peers think, or we can ignore it, and we decide which we do.

◆ We are affected by peer pressure to the extent that our own thinking is already sensitive to the issue we're getting pressured about that we have yet to come to peace with.

◆ We insulate ourselves from peer pressure when we realize that, of course, people will try to get us to do things because of the way they think, and we don't have to take what they think personally.

Sample Questions for Reflective Discussion

Why do you think peer pressure can be such a powerful force for many kids?

What do you think it means that you have "free will?"

What is the only way that peer pressure can affect you?

Do we have to take what other people say to us personally? What is the difference in what happens to you when you take something personally and when you don't?

C. Needed Materials

None

D. Opening Statement

ASK: From your home practice, tell me about the reactions you had to others, and whether you were able to see the grain of truth in the other side.

[Note to teacher: To help the students feel comfortable about discussing this, it would be great if you were able to share a personal reaction that you once had with someone, and at least what you didn't see of that other person's "truth."]

[discussion]

There is nothing wrong with having reactions to others and what they're doing. We all have them. Mostly we can't help the reactions we have. The question is, how seriously do we take these reactions? We could either take them to heart or chalk them up to a low mood or to just the way we happen to be seeing it. Then we can let it go. We don't have a choice about the reactions we get; we only have a choice about what to do with those reactions.

Here is another way to put it: If I have a reaction to someone, do I see the problem as being caused by "the person out there," or do I see the problem as "I must not be seeing something right?" When we have a reaction to someone, at that point we are at that fork in the road. Whichever of those roads we go down will determine the experience we get. When we say, "I must not be seeing something right," we are looking toward our own thinking, and that direction tends to make us feel a little better. When we say, "it's that person," as long as we keep thinking about that person we will feel the same or worse. The same is true about any situation we are having difficulty with.

If someone, however, is abusing us in some way, we also have the wisdom and the free will to take constructive action. We will talk more about free will later in this session as we talk about peer pressure, today's topic.

Most schools have a number of different groupings of friends. Each group appears to be different from the other — from their style of clothing to their behaviors.

ASK: Name all the different groupings of kids in this school [or in high school].

[list on board]

ASK: What does each group look like? Describe them.

[entertain ideas]

ASK: What does each group think about the other groups?

[entertain ideas]

ASK: What does each group think like?

[discussion]

Sometimes from the outside it looks as if everyone within each group looks and acts like a clone of the others in the group. This is because teenagers seem to have a lot of insecurities, since they're trying to figure out who they are in the world. So there is a lot of "following the pack" because following the pack seems to bring a sense of security. Yet, it is only a false sense of security because that person may only be secure when he or she is around their friends.

When adults look back on high school many years later, they often recall a student who stood out from the crowd, who cared very little about how he or she appeared to others. That person just seemed to be on top of life, so she or he was often quite popular. And there are other people who just seem content with doing their own thing, and they don't care much about what anyone else thinks of them.

ASK: Who in this school is like either of those types?

[entertain ideas]

ASK: What do you think they think like?

[discussion]

E. Activity/Story Line

TASK: Divide into groups of four or five *[Note to teacher: Be sure that different peer groups are represented across these groupings.]* Each group is to create its own theory of peer pressure: What makes people follow others, dress like they dress, act like they act, do what they do. Consider what happens within people's thinking.

Then, talk about whether you have ever followed your peers even when you didn't want to do something, and what was going on in your mind when you did this.

Then the other students in the group can offer suggestions on how they might have avoided that dilemma by having different thoughts. What kinds of different thoughts might have been helpful?

[After about 15 minutes in small groups, have discussion in full group]

ASK: What did you learn from this? What do you think is the difference between our true nature and the way we are when we're trying to conform?

[discussion]

By the way, an interesting sidelight is that sometimes when people are trying to be nonconformists, they sometimes end up looking like one another (for example, the hippies of the '60's; the punk crowd, goths, and so on).

TASK: On a piece of paper write down how you think you would look and act if you felt absolutely no pressure from anyone to conform. Be honest with yourselves here. You have about 5 minutes to write this.

ASK: What would school be like for you if there were no peer clique groups?

[discussion]

The good thing about peer groups is that they can be a lot of fun. It's great to have friends. The down side is pressure to conform. Peer pressure can sometimes lead to danger. People can get badly hurt, all because they wanted to fit in, for example, freshmen at colleges who try to fit in by drinking and chugging tons of beer or other alcohol, and they pass out and die.

Many people don't realize that they are often respected more when they rely more on their own true nature. A group of kids may give them a hard time about it, but that is usually because of their own insecurities.

Thinking we need to do something to please others, even when we don't want to do what they are telling us, is some pretty crazy thinking when you stop and think about it.

Peer pressure is just a thought that we can choose to buy into or let go of. This is our free will.

ASK: Here's another point. How can we protect ourselves from peer pressure?

[entertain ideas]

Here's a little situation that may help us think about this.

Let's say that you just had an idea: you realize that your friends have been treating a new kid at school pretty badly, and you have been feeling uncomfortable about it. You decide to tell them to lay off, that everyone deserves to be treated respectfully because that's how they would like to be treated.

You go to your best friend.

"You're kidding, right?" says your friend. "Forget it! You'll just get everyone mad at you if you tell them that."

You go to another friend, who says, "Good idea. I've been thinking the same thing."

You go to another friend. "Get real!"

The leader of your group calls you a wimp (or worse) and says, "We'll treat anybody however we want. Get out of my face!" Most of the group goes along with the leader.

The person you're dating thinks that what you said is wonderful.

No matter what you say, a certain number of people will be in favor of it, and a certain number of people will be against it. It will always be that way. You could have the greatest idea in the world, and some people will think it's a lousy idea. Therefore, when it comes to public opinion, you can't win.

Therefore, you also can't lose.

Your friends and others will put pressure on you to do lots of things, but since you can't win and you can't lose, you may as well just do what you think is right — from a clear head. This also is your free will.

ASK: Let's say a whole bunch of people don't like your idea, and a small percentage of people do like your idea, shouldn't you go along with what most people say?

[discussion]

Nearly everyone in Italy and Spain thought Christopher Columbus's ideas were crazy. If he had listened to everybody else he would never have discovered "the New World." On the other hand, the Native Americans probably wish — with good reason — that Columbus had listened to everyone else and not set sail.

Initially, most established scientists thought that Albert Einstein's ideas were crazy. At first only a handful of scientists listened. If Einstein had listened to most people, he never would have persisted until he discovered his theory of relativity.

A long, long time ago a medical doctor named Ignaz Semmelweiss ordered the medical assistants who worked for him to wash their hands before doing operations (instead of wiping their hands on their smocks) because he thought they were carrying some kind of poison on their hands that was causing infections. Nearly all other medical doctors of the time thought his ideas were crazy. If they couldn't see anything on their hands it wasn't there. They laughed at him and called him crazy. But his ideas led to the discovery of germs (which nobody knew existed before there were microscopes).

History is loaded with great visionaries whose ideas were considered crazy or terrible by the masses of people. But, just because a lot of people are in favor of what you think and a few are against what you think does not mean that you are wrong and the rest are right. What we think is right is all that counts.

Does this mean we shouldn't listen to anyone else? No. We'll talk more about that later.

The key is to know which part of ourselves are we listening to when we want to know what's best to do. Are we listening to Slick or Cool, to our insecure thinking or to our wisdom? That's what really tells us what's right. We just have to get quiet enough to listen to our hearts, so we know which "right" we're listening to. We can tell the difference because listening to wisdom is a deep knowing. Nobody can talk us out of it, we just know.

Seeing this is one step along the way to protecting us from peer pressure.

Here's something else that will help protect us: we think we're being affected by peer pressure, but we're really being affected by our own thinking.

ASK: What do you think this means?

[entertain ideas]

People are only affected by what has meaning to them, personally.

Here is an example: Julie's friends said that she was looking fat. Julie freaked out and stopped eating.

The same group of friends told Cindy that she was looking fat. Cindy looked in the mirror and thought they were crazy.

ASK: What was the difference between Julie and Cindy?

[discussion]

Julie had an issue of being fat that she carried around in her head, in her own thinking. When it got reinforced she let it have a strong effect on her. Cindy didn't have an issue of being fat in her head. It rolled off her like water off a duck's back.

That same group of friends told Julie that she talked too much. Julie smiled. The group told Cindy that she talked too much, and Cindy freaked out. That's what Cindy's parents always told her. She worried about it.

If we have a bad bruise and we're at a dance that's really crowded, and somebody bumps into us, it would hurt. It's not the fault of the person who bumped us because he didn't know about the bruise. What we carry around with us in our heads is sometimes like an emotional bruise that people don't know we have. They might say something that bumps against it, and we feel hurt. The real problem is having the bruise, the emotional bruise, and not the person bumping against it.

If we weren't already carrying around in our head a particular thing that we're worried about, we wouldn't be affected by any peer pressure about that issue. When it hits home, it affects us. So it's not the peer pressure, it's what we're already concerned about that makes us follow others or makes us react. Those things are only thoughts in our heads that we haven't come to peace with yet. The other person is just tempting us to use that thought.

What this all means is that peer pressure is really just an illusion. Unless we think something that lowers our spirits, our spirits are not going to be lowered by others. Unless we think that we're willing to do what other people want us to do, we're not going to do it. It's all inside our own heads — no matter what kind of pressure is "out there."

And that is the greatest power that we have. No one can ever get inside our head and change what we think. That is our free will!

Suppose someone wants us to help them shoplift in a store. If we could only say to ourselves, "Thank you for offering that thought. Now I decide whether to think it myself and whether to let it affect me," we'd be more protected.

Suppose your friend wants to smoke some marijuana. He insists that you do it with him. Your wisdom tells you, "Uh oh, watch it. Something doesn't feel right." You listen to your wisdom and say you're not doing it. He gets mad at you and says "What are you, a chicken or a narc? Either do it or I'm not going to let you hang out with me."

TASK: Ask for volunteers to role play this situation.

Peer Pressure

ASK: How could he not be affected by what his friend said to him?

[discussion]

One way to not be affected is to see that this is how that other person thinks and, because of that, OF COURSE he will try to get you to do stuff, or OF COURSE he will say what he says to you, given the way he thinks. What he says makes perfect sense to him. Given the way he thinks, he has no other choice but to say or do what he says. *We* don't have to get caught up in his stuff.

OF COURSE they'll think that what I'm wearing is weird and make fun of me because they think they all need to dress alike.

This is the kind of thought we have when we are protected from peer pressure.

But sometimes we want to listen to other people whom we trust, and it's good to do that.

ASK: How do we know when to listen to others and when not to?

[discussion]

Our wisdom will tell us if people have our best interests at heart — if we get quiet enough to hear it.

F. Home Practice

Experiment with how you would look and act if there were no pressure to conform to others.

G. Summary/Conclusion

We can think for ourselves or let others think for us. We have the free will to set aside what our peers think, if it makes us uncomfortable. They represent just another set of thoughts.

Session Twenty-Five

What To Do When You May Be Heading Down A Difficult Path

A. To Teachers

This session is intended to serve as a summary of what we have learned thus far, about what to do when our feelings are compelling us to do things that most people would think inadvisable. We will review what emotions are and how they can drive us to destructive behaviors directed toward ourselves or others.

We will also take it one important step further. We need to make the distinction between seeing something as "real," then trying to adjust our thinking about it (as cognitive psychology suggests) vs. calling into question what we see as "real" in the first place. These are very different approaches to life, and we will likely get different results depending on which we follow.

B. Key Points

◆ Destructive cycles can be diminished or stopped by observing how our own thinking is the driving force behind the compelling feelings that get us into difficulty.

◆ To intervene in a destructive cycle, we can recognize that we're not seeing things right, want a change, trust that it can change, quiet our thoughts and listen to what our wisdom tells us, and seek help or support if we need it.

◆ Seeing something as "real" and trying to think differently about it is more difficult to do, and is not as powerful, as calling into question what we see as "real" in the first place.

Sample Questions for Reflective Discussion

Why do you think some people miss all the warning signs as they are heading down a difficult path? Do you think it could help someone if they noticed the warning signs? What are the warning signs?

What do you think it would be helpful to do if you've got a compelling urge that is driving you toward some behavior that, deep in your mind, you know isn't right?

What do you think it means that what we see is what we get?

What can calming the mind, quieting down, clearing the head, do for you when you are experiencing a problem?

C. Needed Materials

overhead/chart/handout #1: stimulus — emotion

overhead/chart/handout #2: stimulus — generated in own mind — emotion

overhead/chart/handout #3: stimulus — observer — different feeling

D. Opening Statement

ASK: Were you able to experiment with how you would look and act if there were no pressure to conform to others? What did you find out?

[discussion]

Today we're going to look at some problems faced by many teenagers and what to do about them.

Whenever we get involved in a problem where we're either feeling horrible inside or we feel like hurting someone or something, it almost feels like we're compelled to either mope around or to take some drastic action just to prove that we are here and that we matter. That powerful feeling is what drives us. It's like we're driven by this feeling that just won't let go.

Sometimes it feels as if some creature is standing over us with a whip and making us do stuff.

It's true: some creature is! The creature is our own powerful emotions inside us. Our emotions are driving us and pushing us. It's like Slick is sitting on our shoulders barking orders into our ears. But its onlu our own thinking doing it to us.

It is humbling to know that we've made up our own set of orders that are now driving us and pushing us and making us do things. Here is how it works:

E. Activity/Story Line

True story: On a driving trip across the country, driving through the Death Valley desert to reach Las Vegas, the three people in the car had not stocked up on enough water, and they ran out. It was blistering hot. They couldn't use their air conditioning because the car was running so hot they were afraid it would overheat and they'd be stuck. The sun beat down on them. They all became extremely thirsty. Meredith, a teenage girl, could not rest until she got some water. She felt like she was going to die! When they finally arrived in Las Vegas she couldn't wait one second before getting something to drink. It was all she could think about.

The two others were very thirsty too, but they enjoyed seeing the sights in Las Vegas as they drove in. They were just glad to be there. They figured they'd get something to drink when they found something.

Meredith didn't even notice that she was in Las Vegas. She could only think about her desperate thirst. Before this she had been so looking forward to seeing Las Vegas. Now she was cranky and irritable and desperate. But she wasn't really any thirstier than the other two. She wasn't in danger. She didn't die. She probably could have been in that state for another whole day or two before her body was really in danger. Yes, the feeling of thirst was giving her an important signal (it works the same way physically or mentally) but that doesn't mean that the entire world has to screech to a halt until it gets quenched. Meredith allowed that compelling feeling of thirst to take her over entirely. It drove her to see nothing but water. It blocked everything else out of her sight.

Finally, she found some water, and drank until her thirst was gone. Then she noticed where she was. "Oh wow, Las Vegas!"

Sometimes we might get the powerful feeling to have some excitement. We're bored and we just want a little fun. Somebody says, "Hey, let's break into this store!" And oh that sounds so exciting we can barely contain ourselves because it's so nasty and so bad, and it would be such a thrill to do it and almost get caught but get away with it. "Oh man, that sounds great!" It becomes just like the thirst.

Or, sometimes we might get this powerful urge to have a banana split but we've been trying to lose weight and we know it's not a good idea, but the thought of that banana split sounds so good that we're ready to jump out of our skin to get one. It's just like the thirst. If losing weight was so important to us, afterwards we might feel so bad about what we did that we might even feel compelled to stick our finger down our throat to get rid of it. We're driven by the feeling.

Or, sometimes we might feel so low and so bad because nothing seems to be working out right and what's the use of living, and what if we were to just do away with ourselves — would anybody care? Or maybe that's what would get people to finally pay attention to us. So that feeling just drives us to want to destroy ourselves — just like the thirst.

Or, sometimes we just get turned on so bad that we've just got to do something sexual, and we've got to relieve this tension somehow, and oh that person over there looks so hot and we've just got to have them or do something or we're going to jump out of our skin!

Or, oh wouldn't it just be great to go find something totally disgusting to gross out these girls.

Or, oh here comes this boy that's really gross — let's tell him something that will really put him down.

Or, hey, let's see what we can do to get this teacher!

Has anyone ever had any of these kinds of urges? [quickly add] No, don't tell me!

Everybody gets some of these kinds of urges or other urges sometimes that are so compelling they'll drive us anywhere — unless we see something beyond the driving feeling. And, here's an interesting thought, at some point our minds will be on something else entirely, and when they are we won't have the urge.

There are two questions involved:

1. Okay, we've just been hit with this extremely compelling urge. It's driving us and pushing us. What are we going to do about it?

2. What if we have this kind of urge all the time — not just a once in a while thing like the above examples, but it happens a lot?

Let's deal with the first one first:

1. What to Do When We've Got a Compelling Urge Driving Us Toward Some Destructive Behavior

TASK: *[Divide the class of students in half.]* We're going to have a debate. Pick any situation that we described earlier, or any other situation that you can think of that you want to play out. Here is what will happen in the debate. One half of the class will play Slick Computerthoughts and say what you think he or she would tell the mind in this situation. The other half of the class will play Cool Receiverthoughts and say what you think he or she would say in this situation.

[Line the students up on both sides of the room and have one makeshift podium set up on each side where one student at a time can step up to and make a statement. One statement is made per side, then one statement from the other side, and go back and forth until one of the teams runs out of ideas.]

The object of the game: Whoever wins the debate gets control of the mind.

Let the debate begin!

**[When the debate is over, ask them which side they think won.
Of course, they will say that their own side won.]**

Actually, whoever got in the last word is the last thought that the mind takes away. Whichever one the mind ends up believing in and acting on is the real winner of the mind in that moment.

Let's summarize what we're really saying through this debate:

The first thing we need to look at is where this emotion is coming from that is driving us. In other words, what is the source of this compelling feeling? When we look at it, whether it seems to be triggered by something out there, or whether it just seems to be coming from in here [point to head], in either case the first thing to remember is that we are getting our compelling, driving feeling from our own thoughts. And because we are the ones who have created these thoughts, we could also uncreate them, or we could create something else, or by seeing it differently we will have created something else, or we can at least decide whether to follow those thought-based urges or to dismiss them or ignore them.

[pull out chart 1: the stimulus → emotion chart. Or write it on the board]

This is really a review of something we talked about before. Let's say we're walking down the hallway and we see someone coming toward us that we don't like. We suddenly get an urge to push him into a locker as we go by. The closer we get, the stronger the urge gets.

At first glance it looks like the urge is being caused by the person. After all, if we didn't see him we wouldn't have that urge. Most people tend to think that the other person out there is the stimulus that causes the urge. When we see that stimulus and we get that urge, it then sometimes feels like some alien space creature has taken over our body and is making us do it. Oh, we just want to do it so bad!

But we're walking with our friends and one friend sees the same kid coming toward us, and he gets the same thought about how much this kid bothers him, but he lets it pass.

Our other friend sees the same kid and doesn't get the feeling of being bothered at all.

[pull out chart 2: stimulus → generated in own mind → emotion]

If the stimulus of the kid were making us feel bothered, everyone who saw this kid would be equally bothered by him — but only some people are. But one friend wasn't bothered as much and our other friend wasn't bothered at all. Therefore, even though it looks to us like it's the kid who makes us bothered, it's not. Something happens in our own head that makes us feel the bother and get the compelling urge to shove him.

If we know that we're the generators of our own compelling emotions through our own thinking, simply knowing that does not allow the compelling urge to have as much of a gripping hold on us.

[pull out chart 3: stimulus → observer → different feeling]

When we observe ourselves having the thoughts that are generating the compelling emotions, it breaks the circuit and takes the power out of it.

Here's our choice: as long as we focus on the other kid, the more the bother stays on our mind. The more air you put into a balloon, the bigger it gets. The more we see our own thinking as the culprit and allow those thoughts to simply flow through and not take hold — the same as letting go of the sharp rock — the less air will be in the balloon and the less power it will have to drive us. The more we realize, "Gee, if I'm bothered this badly, I must not be seeing something right" — we can even be puzzled by it — the more the urge will diminish.

Now let's deal with the second issue:

2. What to Do When We Get a Certain Kind of Urge All the Time

It's really the same problem. The same thing is going on. It's still a debate between Slick and Cool. It's still a thought or series of thoughts in our own heads that are giving us a compelling urge all the time. The only difference is that, for whatever reasons, it happens more often and therefore seems worse.

It may have been because we had or have a lot of bad stuff going on at home, or maybe we had some really bad things happen to us. But that just made us see things in a certain way. It means that our thoughts may be more hurting than some other people's thoughts are. But no matter where they came from, and no matter how strong they are, we still have to realize that they are only our thoughts and only have the power over us that we give them. So it still works like the last chart.

If we think that we need something real bad like that stuff we see in a store that we can't afford, and we often get urges like that, so long as we think that way, then we are going to feel like we really need it bad, and it's going to drive us to try to do something about it. That urge will keep happening over and over again whenever we see similar things that we want — unless we see the source as our own thinking instead of the source as "that thing I see out there."

If we think someone is attractive, that person will be attractive to us. The more we think we want that person, the more we will want them. We might want them so badly that we'll try anything to get them to like us or to pay attention to us. From their view we might be in their face too much or they may think we're obnoxious and it might drive them away. We're trying so hard that it has the opposite effect. But it feels like we can't help it! It looks like it's got to be the attractive person, not my own thinking! But it only looks that way. If it were the attractive person, everyone would have the same urge, and that simply isn't true.

If we get angry so often that we just want to go around punching people in the face or bullying them, we'll feel compelled to do it. "Everybody gets in my way! Everybody is out to get me and my family. They always have been. That's what my father told me and I can see that it's true. We've got to get them before they get us." We keep being driven by those same thoughts over and over again. But the fact is that we are being driven, we are being compelled. That is our signal! That means something isn't right about the way we're seeing it. It's not keeping us in a peaceful, calm state of mind. If we can see that it is our own thinking, it will not have as much grip on us.

So okay, let's say that we do see that our thinking has something to do with that urge to strike first, and we try to do something about our thinking and it doesn't work. It means that we're still not seeing something else. It's great to see that it has something to do with our thinking, but we're still missing something.

Maybe we think that people really do get in our way, and that we'll just try to adjust our thinking so that it doesn't bother us as much. That's a more productive thought than what we had been doing, but there are two problems with it: 1) for most of us that's too hard to do, especially when we've been thinking that way for 13 years; 2) the real problem is the fact that we think the problem is real. In other words, we're saying to ourselves, "Given the fact that people are out to get me, how can I think differently?" As long as we see that the problem is "people are out to get me" we will always have to be fighting our thoughts in reaction to it.

The real shift in thinking comes when we call into question the very "fact" that people are out to get us. We just have to be open to the possibility that it may not be true, that the very "fact" itself is also caused by our own thinking, that if we didn't see it that way it wouldn't be that way, and it wouldn't be "true" or "real." If we saw it differently in the first place, we wouldn't have any further thinking to "try" to adjust.

Does this mean we should "try" to see it differently? It's not bad to try, but we can't expect it to work because trying to think differently — think our way out of a habit — is so hard to do. What we need to do in this case is just know that the way we're seeing it may not be the way it "is" and if we're getting compelling urges that keep us in a low or mean or agitated or angry state, hope that we'll see it differently sometime. And we know that we've got it in us to see it differently, and have faith in that possibility. It may not happen overnight, but if we're pointed in that direction we may be surprised at what can change. The possibility is what keeps the hope of the new alive, and the possibility is always there because it is only thought, and thought is the most changeable thing there is.

This concept also holds for people who think that life is so hard or that life is a drag and that it's always going to be a drag, it's always going to be depressing. The more terrible or burdensome we think life is the more terrible and burdensome it gets for us — sometimes to the point where we just don't want to live any more. If we think it's really that way, it is that way — for us. If we thought that life was really another way, it would be that way — for us. That's the awesome power of thought. It's the power to change our very lives!

Nothing could be more awesome! That our wisdom is always there to guide us is the greatest gift to humankind, and everyone has equal ability to find it in themselves.

ASK: How do you know the difference between what your wisdom and common sense is saying to you and what your Slick thoughts are telling you?

[discussion]

They sound different. Remember, cool wisdom and common sense will sound like fresh ideas that feel right in our hearts. Slick thoughts usually sound like the same old things that are driving us all the time.

The biggest decision we can ever make in life is which voice we listen to.

And if we can't get quiet enough to hear it or still feel compelled to do stuff we know isn't right or doesn't feel good afterwards, even after knowing all this, rather than act on it, we need to find someone who can give us help. That is extremely important.

F. Home Practice

When you get an urge to do something, practice seeing if you can tell the difference between the contaminated thinking you get from Slick, and the wise free-flowing thoughts you get from Cool.

And when you get the urge-type thoughts, see if you can keep letting those thoughts go, dismissing them or ignoring them or whatever you need to do with them, until you reach a deeper and deeper state of quiet. Try it. It's kind of like mediation, but it's something you can do any time and any place.

emotion

stimulus

emotion

generated in own mind

stimulus

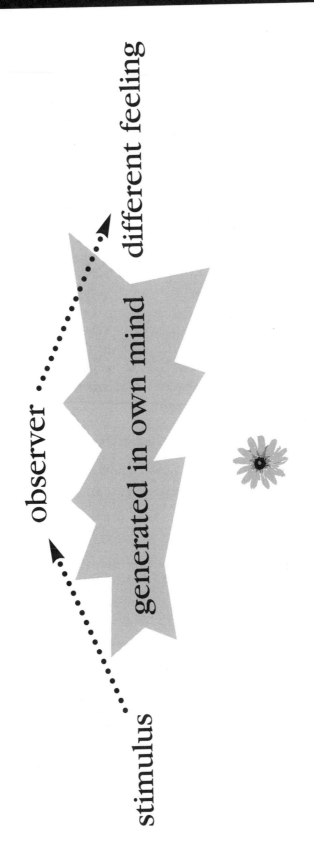

Session Twenty-Six

Summary and Conclusions:
Taking Responsibility For Our Own Lives

A. To Teachers

This entire curriculum has attempted to show how, without our knowing it, thought controls the feelings we have in life, what we get from life, and what we do.

No realization could be more powerful.

The problem is, we cannot simply say the words. We have to discover its true meaning for ourselves. So do the students. The purpose of this curriculum was to put people in a position where they can make such a discovery.

Some students may not have. Yet, because of what the students learned it is possible that some of them may discover it later: "Oh that's what they were talking about!" Or, they may never discover it. But even if they picked up one little thing that protects them from being lost in the ravages of life, their lives will be a little better off.

To summarize it in a nutshell, our mind generates thoughts that are brought to life through our consciousness as picked up by our senses, which in turn gives us an experience of life. Through our thoughts, each of us picks up things differently and we see things differently at different times depending on our moods. Thus we each create our own separate worlds that seem "real" which we then live in and react to. But it is always possible to see at different levels of understanding.

All of us are capable of seeing that we have this clear, healthy place inside of us that can be tapped and can give us the answers we seek in life. All of us are capable of realizing that when our conditioned, processing, busy, computer thinking calms down or shuts off, we can hear our wisdom and common sense. It's there for everyone.

There's a saying in the Midwest: "If you want the water to run clear, you have to get the hogs out of the stream."

If we want our inner health to rise to the surface, the misguided thoughts that are keeping it muddied need to clear. We can help it clear if we see the mechanism behind it. That was the purpose of this curriculum.

The key to understanding lies in the feeling, not in intellectual understanding.

It is like riding a bike. It's hard when we start, but afterwards it's effortless and thought-less.

The best way to find this understanding is to be grateful for what we do have, and when we feel ourselves becoming upset, take responsibility for it by knowing that the upet is coming from us.

B. Key Points

◆ We are all born with perfect mental health inside us, which contains wisdom and common sense, and which we can access through a clear mind.

◆ This health can be obscured by a separate way of thinking that takes us away from experiencing that health and colors the way we see and thus experience life.

◆ Our feelings tell us if we're on the right track. The moment we feel ourselves being upset or angry or fearful, we can take responsibility for our own thinking, be open to the possibility that we're getting faulty messages, and see the possibility of new thought, new sight, and thus new experience.

C. Needed Materials

Coloring materials, paper to draw or color on.

Evaluation forms, and pencils or pens.

If possible, set up your classroom in a large circle for this session, or a staggered double-row circle if there is not enough room.

D. Opening Statement

This is the last of these sessions in this curriculum. We hope it has been useful to you.

The only thing that really matters is whatever learning you got for yourselves, whatever insights you gain for yourselves. So that is what we are going to explore today.

E. Activity/Story Line

Okay, everyone clear your minds!

ASK: Draw how the mind works — in whatever way you think of it.

[Remind the students that there is no right way or wrong way to express their ideas. Expression is unique to each individual. They can be as creative in their expression as they want to be. Give ten or fifteen minutes for this activity]

ASK: Does anyone want to share their drawings with the full class and explain what it means?

[It would be nice if everyone clapped or somehow showed support for each person's drawings and explanation. Then, collect them. In a week or so the teacher should hand them out to the students again so they can keep them as reminders to themselves.]

ASK: Now, clear your minds again. What did you learn most from these sessions that you didn't know before? Keep your mind clear and when something comes to you, when it pops up in you, write it down on this form [hand out evaluation forms]. You don't have to put your name on this if you don't want to.

[give them five or ten minutes for this]

ASK: Let's go around the room and have people share one thing that you learned from this course.

[let anyone pass who wants to, but only if they ask to]

[collect the papers]

[TELL them your own feelings about doing this curriculum, and what it was like for you to teach it, and that hopefully they will all help each other keep these things in mind as they go through the rest of the school year.]

[go over the summary/conclusions below]

F. Home Practice

Remember, this is your life, so the more you keep these things in mind, no matter what you do, the better off you will likely be.

G. Summary/Conclusion

As you go through life, you can each create the kind of world for yourself that you want to live in, because you are really living your thoughts, and those thoughts are always changing. and with it, what you experience of life."

The question is always to be aware of whether you are listening to Slick or to Cool at any given time — which, remember, is really just your own thinking — and decide who you can trust.

The more you use your feelings as your own guides, to tell you whether they are on or off track the better off you will likely be.

The more you take responsibility for what you feel and do (because it all comes from what you think) the better off you will likely be.

The more you can quiet or clear your mind so you can tap into the wisdom inside you, the better off you will likely be. It is always there to guide you, but it can only help you if you listen to it.

Don't worry if you get off track sometimes and forget what you learned. That will happen, it happens to everyone. That's just your mood talking. And it will change. Wisdom lies in even difficult situations when we get off track. It means we're ready to learn something new that we hadn't seen before. There is no failure, just temporary lostness.

Now that you have gone through this with each other, you can help each other keep on track. If you see that someone has temporarily lost it, help them out. Mostly they'll just need someone who cares, who feels good to be around, someone who listens to them. But if the feeling is right, and you see something that they don't see about their thinking, you may be able to gently help them see it. If they don't accept it, that's okay, don't take it to heart. Just continue to see your own thinking and point in the direction of your health and wisdom.

If other people do you wrong or do you harm, know that's only their insecurity talking. You don't have to take it personally.

Life can be so beautiful. You only have to think it, see it, be it.

BIBLIOGRAPHY

Banks, S. (1998). *The missing link*. Vancouver, BC: Lone Pine Publishing.

Bays, L., & Freeman-Longo, R. (1989). *Why did I do it again? Understanding my cycle of problem behaviors: A guided workbook for clients in treatment*. Orwell, VT: Safer Society Press.

Carlson, R., & Bailey, J. (1997). *Slowing down to the speed of life. How to create a more peaceful, simpler life from the inside-out*. New York: Harper-Collins.

Carpenos, L. (1988). Understanding stress. *Prentice-Hall Business & Law Journal*.

Freeman-Longo, R., & Pithers, W.D. (1992). *A structured approach to preventing relapse: A guide for sex offenders* [video]. Brandon, VT: Safer Society Press.

Gray, A.S., & Ziegler, D. (1991/1993). *Breaking sticky thinking: Thinking errors*. Burlington, VT: Vermont Center for the Prevention and Treatment of Sexual Abuse/STEP Program.

Gorski, T.T., & Miller, M. (1986). *Staying sober: A guide for relapse prevention*. Independence, MO: Herald House/Independence Press.

Lester, J. (1999 Reprint Edition). *The Tales of Uncle Remus: The Adventures of Brer Rabbit*. New York: Penguin/Puffin.

Mills, R.C. (1997). *Realizing mental health*. New York: Sulzberger & Graham.

Mills, R.C. (1991). A new understanding of self: Affect, state of mind, self-understanding, and intrinsic motivation. *Journal of experimental education*. 60: 67–81.

Mills, R.C., Dunham, R., & Alpert, G. (1988). Working with high-risk in prevention and early intervention programs: Towards a comprehensive wellness model. *Adolescence* 23:643–660.

Peck, N., Law, A., & Mills, R.C. (1987). *Dropout prevention: What we have learned*. Ann Arbor, MI: ERIC Clearinghouse.

Pransky, G. (1998). *The renaissance of psychology*. New York: Sulzberger & Graham.

Pransky, G. (1990). *The relationship handbook* [a.k.a. *Divorce is not the answer*]. Blue Ridge Summit, PA: TAB Books.

Pransky, G. (1991–1999). Practical psychology audio and video tape series (many tapes on many subjects). La Conner, WA: Pransky & Associates, (360) 466–5200.

Pransky, J. (March, 1993). Interview with Robert Freeman-Longo on the mind of the sexual abuser. *Child Protection Connection*. Waterbury, VT: Department of Social and Rehabilitation Services.

Pransky, J. (1998). *Modello: A story of hope for the inner-city and beyond: An inside-out model of prevention and resiliency in action through Health Realization*. Cabot, VT: NEHRI Publications.

Pransky, J. (1997/1998). *Parenting from the heart*. Cabot, VT: NEHRI Publications.

Stewart, D.L. (1993). *Creating the teachable moment*. Blue Ridge Summit, PA: TAB Books.

For other Health Realization or Psychology of Mind materials or information, see website: www.pombr.com.

Note: Training in the use of this curriculum and in Health Realization is available through Jack Pransky of the NorthEast Health Realization Institute (802) 563-2730, and from Lori Carpenos (860) 668-6882.

Select Safer Society Publications

Roadmaps to Recovery: A Guided Workbook for Young People in Treatment by Timothy J. Kahn (1999). $18.

Pathways: A Guided Workbook for Youth Beginning Treatment by Timothy J. Kahn (Revised Edition 1997). $15.

Pathways Guide for Parents of Youth Beginning Treatment by Timothy J. Kahn (Revised Edition 1997). $8.

STOP! Just for Kids: For Kids with Sexual Touching Problems Adapted by Terri Allred and Gerald Burns from original writings of children in a treatment program (1997). $15.

The Relapse Prevention Workbook for Youth in Treatment by Charlene Steen (1993). $15.

Tell It Like It Is: A Resource for Youth in Treatment by Alice Tallmadge with Galyn Forster (1998). $15.

Feeling Good Again by Burt Wasserman (1999). A treatment workbook for boys and girls ages 6 and up who have been sexually abused. $16.

Feeling Good Again Guide for Parents & Therapists by Burt Wasserman (1999). $8.

When Children Abuse: Group Treatment Strategies for Children with Impulse Control Problems by Carolyn Cunningham and Kee MacFarlane (1996). $28.

From Trauma to Understanding: A Guide for Parents of Children with Sexual Behavior Problems by William D. Pithers, Alison S. Gray, Carolyn Cunningham, and Sandy Lane (1993). $5.

Shining Through: Pulling It Together After Sexual Abuse by Mindy Loiselle and Leslie Bailey Wright (1997). $14. For girls aged 10 and up. New material on body image, self-esteem, self-talk, and sexuality.

Back on Track: Boys Dealing with Sexual Abuse by Leslie Bailey Wright and Mindy Loiselle (1997). $14. A workbook for boys ages 10 and up. Foreword by David Calof.

Adolescent Sexual Offender Assessment Packet by Alison Stickrod Gray and Randy Wallace (1992). $8.

Female Adolescent Sexual Abusers: An Exploratory Study of Mother-Daughter Dynamics with Implications for Treatment by Marcia T. Turner and Tracey N. Turner (1994). $18.

Man-to-Man, When Your Partner Says NO: Pressured Sex & Date Rape by Scott A. Johnson (1992). $6.50.

The Secret: Art & Healing from Sexual Abuse by Francie Lyshak-Stelzer (1999). $22.

Outside Looking In: When Someone You Love Is in Therapy by Patrice Moulton and Lin Harper (1999). $20.

Web of Meaning: A Developmental-Contextual Approach in Sexual Abuse Treatment by Gail Ryan & Associates (1999). $22.

Female Sexual Abusers: Three Views by Patricia Davin, Ph.D., Teresa Dunbar, Ph.D., and Julia Hislop, Ph.D. (1999). $22.

Cultural Diversity in Sexual Abuser Treatment: Issues and Approaches edited by Alvin Lewis, Ph.D. (1999). $22.

When You Don't Know Who to Call: A Consumer's Guide to Selecting Mental Health Care by Nancy Schaufele and Donna Kennedy (1998). $15.

Sexual Abuse in America: Epidemic of the 21st Century by Robert E. Freeman-Longo and Geral T. Blanchard (1998). $20.

Assessing Sexual Abuse: A Resource Guide for Practitioners edited by Robert Prentky and Stacey Bird Edmunds (1997). $20.

Impact: Working with Sexual Abusers edited by Stacey Bird Edmunds (1997). $15.

Supervision of the Sex Offender by Georgia Cumming and Maureen Buell (1997). $25.

A Primer on the Complexities of Traumatic Memories of Childhood Sexual Abuse: A Psychobiological Approach by Fay Honey Knopp and Anna Rose Benson (1997). $25.

The Last Secret: Daughters Sexually Abused by Mothers by Bobbie Rosencrans (1997). $20.

Men & Anger: Understanding and Managing Your Anger for a Much Better Life by Murray Cullen and Rob Freeman-Longo. Revised and updated, new self-esteem chapter (1996). $15.

When Your Wife Says No: Forced Sex in Marriage by Fay Honey Knopp (1994). $7.

Protocol for Phallometric Assessment: A Clinician's Guide by Deloris T. Roys and Pat Roys (1999). $10.

Who Am I & Why Am I in Treatment? A Guided Workbook for Clients in Evaluation and Beginning Treatment by Robert Freeman-Longo and Laren Bays (1988; 8th printing 1997). First workbook in a series of four for adult sex offenders. Also available in Spanish. $12.

Why Did I Do It Again? Understanding My Cycle of Problem Behaviors by Laren Bays and Robert Freeman-Longo (1989; 6th printing 1997). Second in the series. $12.

How Can I Stop? Breaking My Deviant Cycle by Laren Bays, Robert Freeman-Longo, and Diane Montgomery-Logan (1990; 5th printing 1997). Third in the series. $12.

Personal Sentence Completion Inventory by L. C. Miccio-Fonseca, Ph.D. (1998). $50, includes ten inventories and user's guide. Additional inventories available in packs of 25 for $25.

The Safer Society Press is part of The Safer Society Foundation, Inc., a 501(c)3 nonprofit national agency dedicated to the prevention and treatment of sexual abuse. We publish additional books, audiocassettes, and training videos related to the treatment of sexual abuse. To receive a catalog of our complete listings, please check the box on the order form (next page) and mail it to the address listed or call us at (802) 247-3132. For more information on the Safer Society Foundation, Inc., visit our website at http://www.safersociety.org.

Order Form

Date: _____

All books shipped via United Parcel Service. Please include a street location for shipping as we cannot ship to a Post Office box address.

Shipping Address:

Name and/or Agency _____

Street Address (no PO boxes) _____

_____

City _____ State _____ Zip _____

Billing Address (if different from shipping address):

Address _____

_____

City _____ State _____ Zip _____

Daytime phone (_____) _____

P.O. # _____

Visa or MasterCard # _____

Exp. Date _____

Signature (FOR CREDIT CARD ORDER) _____

❑ Please send a catalog.

QTY	TITLE	UNIT PRICE	TOTAL COST

All orders must be prepaid. Make checks payable to and mail to:

SaferSocietyPress

**PO BOX 340
BRANDON, VT
05733-0340**

Shipping & Handling

1–5	items	$5
6–10	items	$8
11–15	items	$10
16–20	items	$12
21–25	items	$15
26–30	items	$18
31–35	items	$22
36–40	items	$25
41–50	items	$30
51+	items	$35

Sub Total	
VT residents (only) add sales tax	
Shipping (see box)	
TOTAL	

Phone orders accepted with MasterCard or Visa. Call (802) 247-3132.

VISA   MasterCard

All prices subject to change without notice. No Returns.
Bulk discounts available, please inquire.
Call for quote on rush orders.
❑ Do not add me to your mailing list.